CHOCOLATE DELIGHTS

CHOCOLATE DELIGHTS

Cathy Gill

CONTENTS

ANOTHER BEST-SELLING VOLUME FROM HPBooks®
Publisher: Rick Bailey; Editorial Director: Elaine R. Woodard
Editor: Jeanette P. Egan; Art Director: Don Burton
Book Assembly: Leslie Sinclair
Typography: Cindy Coatsworth, Michelle Carter
Director of Manufacturing: Anthony B. Narducci
Recipe testing by International Cookbook Services: Barbara Bloch,
President; Rita Barrett, Director of Testing; Nancy Strada, Tester

Published by HPBooks, Inc.
P.O. Box 5367, Tucson, AZ 85703 602/888-2150
ISBN 0-89586-346-4
Library of Congress Catalog Card Number 85-68376
© 1985 HPBooks, Inc. Printed in the U.S.A.
1st Printing

Originally published as Chocolate Cooking
© 1984 Hennerwood Publications Limited

Cover Photo: Mocha & Praline Gâteau, page 48

Introduction

Smooth, luscious chocolate, one of the world's great luxuries, can be used to create a great variety of delights. In this book, we cover the whole field of tempting chocolate morsels, from impressive cakes to simple treats, such as candies and cookies.

Sweet & Simple contains a selection of delicious, easily made puddings, sauces and desserts. These are chocolate treats you can whip up in a hurry to impress family and friends. Try the eye-catching *Fruit Split* with a chocolate sauce, page 10, or *Apricot & Chocolate Dream*, page 20, so easy and so good!

Favorite Desserts includes the more exotic and impressive chocolate desserts. There are cheesecakes, pies, soufflés and ice creams that would make a grand finale to any dinner party. Impress your guests with *Soufflé Monte Carlo*, page 22, or *Ginger Charlotte Russe*, page 24. Thrill them with the elegance of *Chocolate Hearts*, page 33, or spoil them with classic *Cream Puffs with Chocolate Sauce*, page 35.

Cakes presents sixteen wonderful cakes with a whole medley of shapes, sizes and flavors. For a really special occasion, try stunning *Meringue Basket*, page 47, or *Chocolate-Strawberry Valentine*, page 44, decorated with fresh strawberries. No chocolate book would be complete without cakes—the chocoholic's delight.

Party Time is a fun chapter. Here is a whole selection of party treats for children and grownups. Try mouthwatering *Chocolate Fudge*, page 54, or the *Coconut-Topped Pyramids*, page 60. For that special birthday party when the cake must be impressive, make one of the spectacular children's fantasy cakes. *Ozzy Owl*, page 64, or *Barney Bee*, page 63, will make any birthday memorable.

Around the World gives you a taste of chocolate treats from other countries. Old favorites, such as *Bûche de Noel*, page 74, and *Truffles*, page 72, are included. We also show that classic desserts can be adapted to make the most of chocolate. Even the great Australian dessert, *Pavlova*, page 68, can be enhanced by the addition of chocolate.

TYPES OF CHOCOLATE

The major difference in the types of chocolate is in the amounts of *chocolate liquor, cocoa butter,* sugar and other flavorings that the chocolate contains. After the cacao beans are fermented, dried, roasted and hulled, *chocolate liquor* is the finished product. It contains approximately 50 percent cocoa butter. To make unsweetened cocoa powder, some of this cocoa butter is removed. Additional cocoa butter is blended with chocolate liquor to make fine chocolates. The quality and specific formula for a type of chocolate will vary from one brand to another. There is a wide price range in chocolates; buy the one dictated by your taste and budget.

Unsweetened Chocolate
This is also known as bitter or baking chocolate. Bitter chocolate contains no sugar; it may replace a proportion of the chocolate used in some recipes for a stronger, slightly bitter flavor.

Bittersweet Chocolate
This is a slightly sweet chocolate that is widely used in baking, desserts and candy. This is also sometimes called sweet chocolate. The amount of sugar will depend on the brand.

Sweet Cooking Chocolate
This is a special blend of chocolate that includes sugar. It is used most often for German Chocolate Cake.

Milk Chocolate
Milk chocolate has a mild chocolate flavor and is the type preferred by most Americans. In addition to sugar, chocolate liquor, cocoa butter and flavorings, dried milk is added during processing.

White Chocolate
White chocolate is not legally chocolate since it contains no chocolate liquor, but only cocoa butter. It also contains sugar, flavorings and dried milk. White chocolate has a higher sugar content than dark chocolate and is usually considered more of a candy than a cooking chocolate. However, it can be used in cooking and is included in a few recipes here. Great care should be taken when cooking with white chocolate. It is difficult to melt; it softens very slowly and is apt to become grainy.

Confectionery Coating
This is often called artificial chocolate or compound chocolate since some or all of the cocoa butter has been replaced by other fats, such as coconut oil or palm oil. Sometimes part of the chocolate liquor is replaced by other flavoring agents. This chocolate is economical and easy to use. It is suitable for dipping, cake frostings and chocolate decorations.

Couverture Chocolate
Couverture chocolate is a richly flavored chocolate with a high proportion of cocoa butter, giving it a glossy appearance and a smooth texture. To melt and set successfully, the chocolate needs to be tempered by repeated heating and cooling. Because it is expensive and difficult to handle, it is normally used only by professional confectioners. There are no recipes using couverture chocolate in this book.

CHOCOLATE DECORATIONS

Chocolate Squares, Triangles & Wedges

Melt 4 ounces chocolate; see box below. Using a long flexible spatula, spread melted chocolate 1/8-inch thick on waxed paper or foil. Let set. When set, trim the edges of the chocolate. Using a ruler, mark out even-sized squares or rectangles. Cut with a thin sharp knife. Cut squares diagonally to make triangles; cut rectangles diagonally to make wedges. Carefully lift onto a flat plate or board lined with parchment paper. Handle as little as possible to prevent melting.

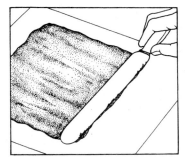

1/Using a long, flexible spatula, spread melted chocolate 1/8-inch thick on waxed paper or foil.

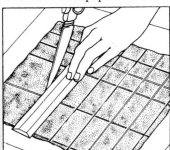

2/Using a ruler, mark out squares or rectangles. Cut with a thin sharp knife.

Melting Chocolate

There are several methods to successfully melt chocolate. Always grate or chop chocolate into pieces before melting. Excess heat causes chocolate to become dry and grainy.

To use a double boiler, place chocolate pieces in the top of a double boiler over barely simmering water. Stir until smooth. Do not get any water drops in the chocolate or it will *seize*, or become hard and grainy. Chocolate that has seized can be saved by stirring in a few teaspoons vegetable shortening, a little at a time.

To use a microwave oven, place chocolate pieces in a small microwave-safe dish. Cook 30 seconds. Check chocolate; chocolate may still look solid but actually be melted. Repeat as many times as needed to almost melt chocolate. Stir until smooth. This method works best with larger amounts of chocolate.

To use a saucepan, melt chocolate pieces in a heavy saucepan over very low heat. Stir until smooth. This method is most successful when additional ingredients, such as butter or margarine, are heated with the chocolate.

Chocolate Leaves

Melt 2 ounces chocolate; see box below. Stir until smooth; cool to 92F to 100F (35C) or until it has a smooth, glossy appearance. Follow the illustrations below.

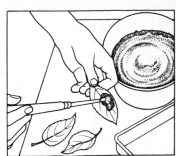

1/Using a brush, spread melted chocolate on underside of dry, clean leaves.

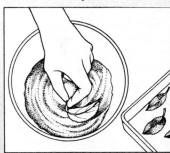

2/Or, dip underside of leaves in melted chocolate. Place on waxed paper to set.

3/When chocolate is firm, carefully peel away leaf, starting at the stem.

Chocolate Curls

Hold a bar of room-temperature chocolate over a plate. Draw the blade of a vegetable peeler along the thin edge of the bar; let the curls fall onto the plate.

Grated Chocolate

Chill chocolate for about 15 minutes. Using the size grater desired, grate chocolate finely or coarsely onto a plate. Hold

the chilled chocolate with a small piece of foil to prevent your fingers from melting the chocolate. Remove foil as the chocolate piece gets smaller.

Chopped Chocolate

Break room-temperature chocolate into squares. Place on a chopping board. With a sharp, heavy knife, chop squares into pieces of desired size.

Chocolate Cut-Out Shapes

Melt 4 ounces chocolate; see box page 7. Using a long flexible spatula, spread melted chocolate 1/8-inch thick on waxed paper or foil. Let set. Stamp out shapes using small cookie or canapé cutters. Leftover chocolate can be melted and used again.

Chocolate Scrolls

Melt unsweetened or semisweet chocolate; see box page 7. Using a long flexible spatula, spread melted chocolate to a thickness of about 1/8 inch on a cool work surface. Cool until set. Push a long heavy knife or heavy metal spatula under the chocolate at a slight angle. Shorter scrolls are formed by pushing the blunt end of a spatula under chocolate.

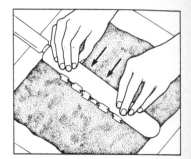

Chocolate Bark

Spread melted chocolate as above; cool until set. Place a long sharp knife on the surface of chocolate; hold the tip of knife securely. Holding the knife at a slight angle, push knife slightly into the chocolate. Scrape in a quarter circle to produce long thin chocolate curls, keeping knife point at the same location. With practice, very long curls can be made.

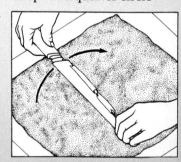

STORING & CHILLING CHOCOLATE

Store chocolate in a cool, dry place. During hot weather all chocolate used for decorations may need to be placed in the refrigerator to set. Chocolate absorbs odors very easily. If you keep chocolate in the refrigerator or freezer for any length of time, wrap it tightly. The grayish-white film or *bloom* that you sometimes see on chocolate is the result of cocoa butter or sugar crystals rising to the surface after exposure to varying temperatures. It does not affect the flavor and disappears when the chocolate is melted.

PIPED DECORATIONS

Rosettes—Use a star or special rosette tip. With tip close to cake surface, pipe icing in a complete circle, ending in the center. Finish off quickly to leave a small raised point.

Stars—Use a star tip. With pastry bag upright and tip close to cake surface, pipe out icing to size of star desired; quickly pull away with a down and then up movement.

Shells—Use a special shell tip or star tip. Pressing lightly on bag and with tip close to cake surface, move the tip away from and then toward you, pressing out more icing for the fat part of the shell.

Scrolls—Use a star tip. With tip close to cake surface, make a question mark with icing, beginning with a thick head and gradually releasing the pressure to make a long tail. Make a second scroll on the tail of the first to form a chain, or reverse design to make double scrolls.

Ropes—Use a plain tip. Pipe icing with a steady pressure to make even ropes and lines.

Ribbons—Use a flat serrated-ribbon tip to make basket designs, ribbons or edgings. To make woven baskets, use a ribbon tip and a plain tip.

To make a parchment-paper pastry bag

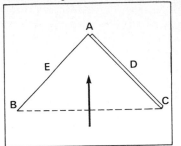

1/Fold a 10-inch square of parchment paper in half to form a triangle.

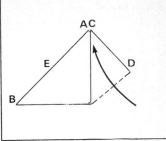

2/Place triangle on a flat surface. Fold point C to point A; crease well.

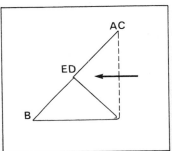

3/Fold point D to point E; crease well.

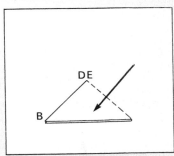

4/Fold point AC to point B; crease well.

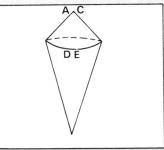

5/Hold bag where points D and E meet. Shape into a cone; fold point AC inside bag.

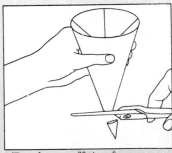

6/Barely cut off tip of cone. Do not fill bag more than half full.

Piping Whipped Cream

Whipped cream for piping can be sweetened or unsweetened. The whipped cream should be stiff enough to hold its shape. Too soft a cream will flatten and not be attractive. Do not overbeat the cream or it will turn into butter and be grainy.

To pipe whipped cream, spoon into a cloth or plastic pastry bag or a parchment-paper pastry bag; see illustrations above. Attach the tip to the pastry bag with a coupling if you want to change tips. Be sure to put the tip or coupling in place before filling the bag! Force the cream out by exerting pressure with your fingers and palm of one hand, while guiding the tip with the other hand.

Sometimes piping will cause the cream to be buttery and uneven. If this happens, discard cream; wash and dry the bag and start again.

Trifle Cake

Cake:
3/4 cup butter or margarine, room temperature
1-1/3 cups sugar
3 eggs
1 teaspoon vanilla extract
1-1/4 cups cake flour
1/2 cup unsweetened cocoa powder
1-1/4 teaspoons baking soda
1/2 teaspoon salt
3/4 cup milk

Topping:
1/4 cup sweet sherry
4 to 6 tablespoons strawberry jam or preserves
2/3 cup whipping cream
1 tablespoon powdered sugar

To decorate:
4 or 5 strawberries, sliced
About 30 small almond macaroons

1. Preheat oven to 350F (175C). Generously grease a deep 8-inch-round cake pan or springform pan.
2. In a medium bowl, beat butter or margarine and sugar until light and fluffy. Beat in eggs and vanilla until blended.
3. Sift flour, cocoa, baking soda and salt into a medium bowl. Add flour mixture to sugar mixture alternately with milk; beat until blended. Pour batter into greased pan; smooth top.
4. Bake in preheated oven 55 to 60 minutes or until a wooden pick inserted in center comes out clean. Cool in pan on a wire rack 5 minutes. Remove from pan; cool completely on wire rack.
5. Place cake, top-side up, on a serving plate. Prick top all over with prongs of a fork. Sprinkle 3 tablespoons sherry over top of cake; let stand 1 hour. Spread jam or preserves over top of cake.
6. In a medium bowl, beat cream until soft peaks form. Beat in powdered sugar and remaining 1 tablespoon sherry. Spread whipped-cream mixture over top of cake. Decorate with strawberries and macaroons. Refrigerate until served. Makes 6 to 8 servings.

Variation
Substitute raspberry, blackberry or other jam for strawberry jam.

Fruit Split

3 oz. semisweet chocolate, broken into pieces
2 tablespoons butter or margarine
2 tablespoons corn syrup
1/4 cup half and half
Juice of 1 lemon
4 small bananas, peeled, halved lengthwise
1/2 cup fresh or canned pineapple chunks, drained
2 kiwifruit, peeled, sliced
8 black grapes, halved, seeded
4 scoops Chunky-Fudge Ice Cream, page 13, or other ice cream, if desired
1/3 cup pine nuts

1. In a small saucepan over low heat, combine chocolate, butter or margarine and corn syrup; stir until mixture is smooth. Cool slightly.
2. Stir in half and half until smooth. Set aside.
3. Squeeze lemon juice over banana halves; place 2 banana halves, rounded-side up, in each individual serving dish.
4. Divide remaining fruit equally among dishes. Top each dish with a scoop of ice cream, if desired.
5. Drizzle warm chocolate sauce over fruit and ice cream. Sprinkle with pine nuts; serve immediately. Pass remaining sauce separately. Makes 4 servings.

Variation
Substitute other fruits for fruit listed above. Sliced strawberries and peaches make a colorful and delicious combination.

Top to bottom: Trifle Cake, Fruit Split

Peach & Caramel Parfait

1/2 cup sugar
1/4 cup water
1/2 cup half and half
1 tablespoon unsweetened cocoa powder
4 large fresh ripe peaches or 8 canned peach halves,
  drained
1 pint butter-pecan ice cream

To decorate:
3/4 cup whipping cream
1/4 cup chopped toasted nuts
4 maraschino cherries
4 chocolate wedges, page 7, if desired

---

1. In a small saucepan over medium heat, stir sugar and water until sugar dissolves. Boil, without stirring, until mixture is a deep golden brown. Remove from heat.
2. While sugar is caramelizing, in a small saucepan over medium heat, blend half and half and cocoa. Bring to a boil. Carefully pour boiling mixture into caramelized sugar. Stir rapidly until caramel is dissolved. Return to heat, if necessary. Let cool.
3. If using fresh peaches, place peaches in a heatproof bowl; cover with boiling water. Let stand 1 minute; plunge peaches into cold water to prevent cooking. Peel off skins. Halve peeled peaches; remove and discard seeds. Cut peaches into quarters.
4. Place alternate layers of peach quarters and scoops of ice cream in 4 tall glasses, ending with a scoop of ice cream. Divide cooled caramel sauce among desserts.
5. To decorate, in a medium bowl, whip cream until soft peaks form. Spoon whipped cream into a pastry bag fitted with a star or rosette tip. Pipe a large rosette of whipped cream on each dessert. Sprinkle with nuts; top each with a cherry. Insert a chocolate wedge beside each cherry, if desired. Serve immediately. Makes 4 servings.

Top to bottom: Peach & Caramel Parfaits, Pineapple with Coconut Sauce

Pineapple with Coconut Sauce

1 fresh medium pineapple, peeled, cored, sliced into 8
  rings
1 tablespoon honey
Juice of 1 lemon
2 tablespoons light rum
2 tablespoons butter or margarine

Coconut Sauce:
2 tablespoons unsweetened cocoa powder
3 tablespoons honey
1/2 cup water
1 tablespoon light rum
2 tablespoons cream of coconut
2 tablespoons half and half
1/2 cup shredded coconut, if desired

1. Place pineapple rings in a large shallow dish. In a small bowl, combine honey, lemon juice and rum; pour over pineapple. Cover and refrigerate overnight.
2. Drain pineapple; reserve marinade. Melt butter or margarine in a large skillet over low heat. Add pineapple; heat through. Do not brown. Transfer to a heated serving dish; keep warm.
3. To make sauce, in a medium saucepan over medium heat, combine reserved marinade, cocoa, honey, water and rum. When hot, stir in cream of coconut and half and half, a little at a time. Stir until smooth.
4. Arrange 2 slices of warm pineapple on each of 4 individual plates. Pour warm sauce over each serving; sprinkle with coconut, if desired. Makes 4 servings.

Chocolate-Cookie Ice Cream

1 pint whipping cream (2 cups)
1/2 cup sugar
1 teaspoon vanilla extract
2 cups chocolate-cookie crumbs (about 38 (2-1/4-inch)
  cookies)
1/2 cup chopped toasted hazelnuts
4 oz. semisweet or sweet chocolate, coarsely chopped

1. In a medium bowl, beat cream, sugar and vanilla until blended.
2. Pour into an ice-cream container. Freeze in an ice-cream maker according to manufacturer's directions until almost firm.
3. Add cookie crumbs, hazelnuts and chocolate to partially frozen ice cream. Freeze until firm. Makes about 1-1/2 quarts or 6 to 8 servings.

Chunky-Fudge Ice Cream

Fudge:
2 tablespoons butter or margarine
2 oz. semisweet chocolate, broken into pieces
1 tablespoon milk
1 cup powdered sugar, sifted
1 teaspoon vanilla extract

Chocolate Ice Cream
1/2 cup water
1/2 cup firmly packed light-brown sugar
2 tablespoons unsweetened cocoa powder
4 egg yolks, beaten
1-1/2 cups half and half or whipping cream
1 teaspoon vanilla extract
1/4 cup chopped toasted almonds

1. Line an 8-inch-square pan with waxed paper. To make fudge, in a small saucepan over low heat, combine butter or margarine, chocolate and milk; stir until smooth. Beat in powdered sugar until smooth. Stir in vanilla. Spoon chocolate mixture into lined pan. Refrigerate about 20 minutes or until set.
2. When chocolate mixture is set, invert on a flat surface. Remove paper; coarsely chop. Set aside.
3. To make ice cream, in a small saucepan over medium heat, combine water and sugar. Stir until sugar dissolves. Boil 5 minutes, without stirring. Beat in cocoa.
4. Pour hot syrup in a steady stream into yolks, beating constantly. Continue beating until cool. Mixture should be light and creamy.
5. Beat half and half into cooled egg-yolk mixture. Stir in vanilla. Pour mixture into an ice-cream container. Freeze in an ice-cream maker according to manufacturer's directions until almost firm.
6. Stir chopped fudge and almonds into partially frozen ice cream. Freeze until firm. Makes about 2 quarts or 6 to 8 servings.

Pears with Chocolate-Maple Sauce

3/4 cup sugar
6 cups water
1 (3-inch) cinnamon stick
4 large ripe pears, peeled
1-1/2 cups chocolate-cake crumbs
1/4 cup chopped walnuts
3 maraschino cherries, chopped
1 to 2 tablespoons maraschino-cherry syrup

Sauce:
1/2 cup maple syrup
1 tablespoon unsweetened cocoa powder

To decorate:
Chocolate leaves, page 7, if desired

1. Preheat oven to 350F (175C). In a large saucepan over medium heat, combine sugar and water. Cook, stirring, until sugar dissolves. Add cinnamon and pears; cover and simmer about 20 minutes or until pears are barely tender when pierced with a skewer at widest part of pear. Cool in sugar syrup.
2. Cut a slice from blossom end of cooled pears so they will stand upright. Cut off about 1 inch of pear at stem to form a top; reserve tops. Scoop out core with a teaspoon or melon baller.
3. In a small bowl, combine cake crumbs, walnuts and cherries; stir in enough cherry syrup to make a stiff paste. Spoon mixture into pear cavities. Replace tops.
4. To make sauce, in a small saucepan over medium heat, blend syrup and cocoa. Bring to a boil, stirring constantly. Pour a little sauce into individual serving dishes; place a filled pear in middle of sauce. Decorate with chocolate leaves, if desired. Makes 4 servings.

Left to right: Pears with Chocolate-Maple Sauce, Lemon Crunch, Apricot-Chocolate Delight

Lemon Crunch

1 teaspoon unflavored gelatin powder
Grated peel and juice of 2 lemons
1/2 pint whipping cream (1 cup)
5 tablespoons superfine sugar
1 cup chocolate-cookie crumbs (about 18 (2-1/4 inch) cookies)
1/3 cup chopped toasted almonds

To decorate:
Shaved chocolate or chocolate curls, page 7

1. In a small saucepan, combine gelatin and lemon juice. Stir well; let stand 3 minutes. Stir over low heat until gelatin dissolves; let cool.
2. In a medium bowl, beat cream until soft peaks form. Beat in sugar. Fold in cooled gelatin mixture and lemon peel until blended. Refrigerate 1 to 2 hours or until mixture mounds when dropped from a spoon.
3. In a small bowl, combine cookie crumbs and almonds. Spoon alternate layers of crumb mixture and lemon cream into a serving bowl, ending with a layer of lemon cream. Refrigerate until served. Decorate with chocolate before serving. Makes 4 servings.

Apricot-Chocolate Delight

16 oz. plain or vanilla-flavored yogurt (2 cups)
1/2 cup muesli, page 78
1/2 cup chopped toasted hazelnuts
2 tablespoons honey
1 (8-oz.) pkg. dried apricots, finely chopped (about
    1-2/3 cups)
4 oz. semisweet chocolate, chopped
2 tablespoons butter or margarine

To decorate:
Chocolate curls, page 7

1. In a medium bowl, combine yogurt, muesli and hazelnuts. Stir in honey. Fold in apricots. Cover and refrigerate 30 minutes.
2. Melt chocolate and butter or margarine in a small heavy saucepan over very low heat; stir until smooth. Cool to room temperature.
3. Place a heaping tablespoon yogurt mixture in bottom of each of 4 individual serving glasses or parfait dishes. Top each dish with 2 to 3 teaspoons melted chocolate, swirling chocolate to outside edge of glass.
4. Spoon remaining yogurt and chocolate alternately into each glass, ending with chocolate. Refrigerate until served. Decorate with chocolate curls before serving. Makes 4 servings.

Chocolate-Banana Pie

Crust:
1-1/2 cups vanilla-cookie crumbs or chocolate-cookie
  crumbs (about 33 cookies)
5 tablespoons butter or margarine, melted

Filling:
4 medium bananas
1 (14-oz.) can sweetened condensed milk
2 teaspoons grated lemon peel
1 (1/4-oz.) envelope unflavored gelatin (1 tablespoon)
About 1/4 cup lemon juice
3/4 cup water
4 oz. semisweet chocolate, chopped
2 tablespoons butter or margarine

1. Preheat oven to 375F (190C). In a small bowl, combine cookie crumbs and melted butter or margarine. Press crumbs on bottom and up side of an 8-inch fluted quiche pan or pie pan.
2. Bake in preheated oven 10 minutes. Cool on a wire rack.
3. Cut 2 bananas into pieces. Reserve remaining bananas for topping. In a blender or food processor fitted with a steel blade, process banana pieces and 2/3 cup condensed milk until bananas are pureed. Pour into a medium bowl; stir in lemon peel.
4. In a small saucepan, combine gelatin, 2 tablespoons lemon juice and water. Stir well; let stand 3 minutes. Stir over low heat until gelatin dissolves; cool slightly. Stir cooled gelatin into banana puree. Spoon banana puree into cooled crust; smooth top. Refrigerate 1 hour or until set.
5. In a medium saucepan over low heat, combine remaining condensed milk, chocolate and butter or margarine. Cook, stirring, until chocolate melts and mixture is smooth. Cool slightly.
6. Pour chocolate mixture over chilled pie, covering banana filling completely. Refrigerate 2 hours or until set.
7. To serve, slice remaining bananas. In a small bowl, toss slices with lemon juice to coat. Arrange slices around edge of pie. Refrigerate until served. Makes 6 servings.

Clockwise from left: Chocolate-Banana Pie, Chocolate Syllabub, Raspberry & Lychee Delight

Chocolate Syllabub

1/3 cup sweet sherry
1 tablespoon brandy
1/4 cup chocolate-flavored drink mix
1/2 pint whipping cream (1 cup)
2 tablespoons powdered sugar
4 oz. semisweet or sweet chocolate, finely grated
2 egg whites

To decorate:
Grated semisweet or sweet chocolate

---

1. In a small bowl, combine sherry and brandy. Stir in drink mix until dissolved and mixture is smooth.
2. In a medium bowl, beat cream until soft peaks form. Beat in powdered sugar. Fold chocolate into whipped-cream mixture. Fold in sherry mixture.
3. In a medium bowl, beat egg whites until stiff but not dry. Fold beaten egg whites into chocolate-cream mixture.
4. Spoon mixture into 4 tall wine glasses. Refrigerate 1 to 2 hours or until served. Decorate with grated chocolate. Serve with cookies, if desired. Makes 4 servings.

Raspberry & Lychee Delight

1/4 cup butter or margarine
2-1/2 cups fresh bread crumbs
2 tablespoons light-brown sugar
1 teaspoon ground cinnamon
Grated peel of 1 orange
5 oz. semisweet chocolate, finely grated
1-1/2 cups fresh raspberries
1 (20-oz.) can lychees, well drained, chopped

---

1. Melt butter or margarine in a medium skillet. Add bread crumbs; cook, stirring, until crisp and golden brown. Cool to room temperature.
2. In a medium bowl, combine cooled bread crumbs, brown sugar, cinnamon, orange peel and 1/3 of chocolate.
3. Set 12 raspberries aside for decoration. Spoon a layer of crumb mixture in bottom of a 3-cup glass serving dish. Top with a layer of raspberries and lychees. Repeat with remaining crumb mixture, raspberries and lychees. Sprinkle with remaining chocolate, covering top completely. Decorate with reserved raspberries. Refrigerate until served. Makes 4 to 6 servings.

White-Chocolate & Strawberry Fondue

Fondue:
1/4 cup butter or margarine
12 oz. white chocolate
1/4 cup half and half
2 tablespoons strawberry-flavored liqueur or raspberry-flavored liqueur

To serve:
Marshmallows
Pound-cake or angel-food-cake cubes
Banana chunks
Pineapple chunks
Fresh strawberries, washed, hulled

---

1. In a medium saucepan over low heat, melt butter or margarine and chocolate; stir until smooth.
2. Stir in half and half and liqueur.
3. Pour into a fondue pot. Keep warm over low heat.
4. Serve with marshmallows, cake cubes, banana chunks, pineapple chunks and strawberries. Use fondue forks or wooden skewers for dipping items into warm fondue. Makes 4 servings.

Mocha Dessert Cups

5 oz. semisweet chocolate, coarsely chopped
1/4 cup butter or margarine, room temperature
1/4 cup sugar
2/3 cup milk
1 egg
1 teaspoon instant coffee powder
2 cups small almond macaroons
2 tablespoons coffee-flavored liqueur

To decorate:
1/4 cup whipping cream, lightly whipped, if desired

This is a simple dessert that can be made ahead of time and refrigerated. Serve with small whipped-cream-filled almond macaroons, if desired.

1. Melt chocolate in a small heavy saucepan over very low heat; stir until smooth. Let cool.
2. In a medium bowl, beat butter or margarine and sugar until light and fluffy. Beat in cooled chocolate until blended. Set aside.
3. In a small bowl, whisk milk and egg until blended. Pour through a fine sieve into a small saucepan; stir in coffee. Cook over low heat, stirring constantly, until sauce thickens and coats back of a spoon. Do not boil. Cool slightly.
4. Gradually pour warm custard into chocolate mixture, beating constantly. Refrigerate 2 hours or until thickened.
5. Place almond macaroons in a medium bowl; sprinkle with coffee liqueur. Let stand 30 minutes.
6. Spoon 1/2 of chilled chocolate mixture into 4 individual serving dishes. Place liqueur-soaked macaroons over mixture. Spoon remaining chocolate mixture evenly over macaroons. Refrigerate 2 hours. To serve, decorate each dessert with 1 tablespoon cream, if desired. Makes 4 servings.

Chocolate Crepes with Rum & Raisin Sauce

Crepes:
1/2 cup all-purpose flour
1/4 cup unsweetened cocoa powder
1/4 cup sugar
2 eggs
1 cup milk
2 tablespoons butter or margarine, melted
Butter or margarine for cooking

Rum & Raisin Sauce:
3 oz. semisweet or sweet chocolate, coarsely chopped
3/4 cup half and half
2 tablespoons dark rum
1/3 cup raisins
Powdered sugar

1. To make crepes, sift flour and cocoa into a medium bowl; stir in sugar.
2. In a small bowl, beat eggs and milk until blended. Beat egg mixture into flour mixture with a whisk until blended. Gradually beat in butter or margarine. Or, combine all ingredients in a blender or food processor fitted with a steel blade; process until batter is smooth.
3. Pour crepe batter into a pitcher; refrigerate 1 hour.
4. Melt 1 teaspoon butter or margarine in a 6- or 7-inch crepe pan or skillet over medium heat. Stir crepe batter. Pour 2 to 3 tablespoons batter into skillet, or enough batter to make a thin layer. Tilt pan from side to side to spread batter evenly. Cook 1 minute or until tiny bubbles form on surface of crepe. Turn crepe; cook 1 minute.
5. Remove crepe; place on a flat plate. Repeat with remaining batter, adding more butter or margarine to pan as necessary.
6. To make sauce, in a small heavy saucepan over low heat, combine chocolate and half and half. Cook, stirring, until chocolate melts and mixture is smooth. Remove from heat; stir in rum and raisins.
7. Fold each crepe into quarters. Place 4 folded crepes on each serving plate. Sift powdered sugar over crepes; spoon some sauce over each serving. Serve remaining sauce separately. Makes 4 to 6 servings or 16 to 24 crepes.

Variation
Whiskey & Walnut Sauce: Substitute 2 tablespoons rye whiskey for rum. Substitute 1/3 cup chopped walnuts for raisins.

Clockwise from left: Chocolate Soufflé Omelet, Chocolate Crepes
with Rum & Raisin Sauce, Cream-filled macaroons, Mocha
Dessert Cups

Chocolate Soufflé Omelet

2 eggs, separated
3 tablespoons chocolate-flavored drink mix
2 tablespoons milk
2 teaspoons grated orange peel, if desired
1 tablespoon butter or margarine

To serve:
Orange marmalade or Special Chocolate Sauce, page 21

To decorate:
Julienned orange peel or grated chocolate

1. In a medium bowl, beat egg yolks, drink mix and milk until blended. Fold in orange peel, if desired.
2. In a medium bowl, beat egg whites until stiff but not dry. Fold beaten egg whites into chocolate mixture. Preheat broiler.
3. Melt butter or margarine in an 8-inch ovenproof skillet or omelet pan over medium heat until bubbly. Pour in chocolate mixture; spread evenly with a long flat spatula.
4. Cook until underside of omelet is set. Cook under preheated broiler, about 3 inches from heat, until top is almost firm.
5. Spoon marmalade or Special Chocolate Sauce over 1/2 of omelet; fold omelet in half. With a spatula, slide filled omelet onto a serving plate. Decorate with orange peel or grated chocolate. Serve immediately. Makes 2 servings.

Chocolate & Apricot Dream

3 tablespoons unsweetened cocoa powder
2 tablespoons cornstarch
3/4 cup granulated sugar
1-1/4 cups milk
2 egg yolks, beaten
1 (17-oz.) can apricot halves, well drained
2 tablespoons apricot brandy
1/2 pint whipping cream (1 cup)
2 tablespoons powdered sugar

To decorate:
Chocolate triangles, page 7

1. In a medium saucepan, combine cocoa, cornstarch and granulated sugar. Gradually stir in milk. Cook over medium heat, stirring, until mixture thickens and comes to a boil. Remove from heat.

2. Stir 1/4 cup hot milk mixture into egg yolks until blended. Return mixture to saucepan; stir well. Cook, stirring, until thickened. Do not boil. Pour chocolate custard into a medium bowl. Cool slightly.

3. Set 2 apricot halves aside for decoration. In a blender or food processor fitted with a steel blade, process remaining apricots until pureed. Stir apricot puree and brandy into cooled chocolate custard.

4. Cover surface of custard with a sheet of waxed paper to prevent a skin from forming. Refrigerate 1 hour.

5. In a medium bowl, beat cream until soft peaks form. Beat in powdered sugar. Spoon 2/3 cup whipped-cream mixture into a pastry bag fitted with a star or rosette tip; refrigerate. Fold remaining whipped-cream mixture into chocolate mixture. Pour into a 4-cup serving bowl; smooth top. Refrigerate until served.

6. To serve, pipe chilled whipped-cream mixture into rosettes on top of chocolate mixture. Cut reserved apricots into thin slices. Decorate rosettes with apricot slices and chocolate triangles. Makes 6 to 8 servings.

Chocolate & Apricot Dream

Chocolate-Butterscotch Sauce

1/3 cup firmly packed light-brown sugar
2 tablespoons chocolate-flavored drink mix
1/4 cup butter or margarine
3/4 cup milk

1. In a small saucepan over low heat, combine brown sugar, drink mix and butter or margarine. Cook, stirring, until sugar dissolves.
2. Increase heat to medium; cook 2 minutes.
3. Remove from heat; stir in milk. Return to heat; boil 2 minutes. Serve warm or cover and refrigerate until chilled. Makes about 1 cup.

Special Chocolate Sauce

4 oz. semisweet chocolate, broken into pieces
1/2 cup half and half
1/4 cup butter or margarine, cubed
2 egg yolks
1 tablespoon strong coffee
1 tablespoon rum

1. In a small saucepan over low heat, combine chocolate and half and half. Cook, stirring, until mixture is smooth. Do not boil.
2. Remove from heat; slowly beat in butter or margarine, 1 piece at a time, until melted.
3. Beat in remaining ingredients until smooth. Serve warm or cover and refrigerate until chilled. Makes about 1 cup.

Fudge Sauce

3 oz. semisweet chocolate, broken into pieces
2 tablespoons butter or margarine
1 (5.3-oz.) can evaporated milk
1/3 cup firmly packed light-brown sugar
1/4 teaspoon vanilla extract

1. In a medium saucepan over low heat, combine all ingredients. Cook, stirring, until chocolate melts and sugar dissolves. Do not boil.
2. Serve hot or warm. Makes about 1 cup.

Quick Chocolate Sauce

2 tablespoons unsweetened cocoa powder
1/4 cup corn syrup or honey
1/4 cup butter or margarine
1/2 cup milk
1/2 teaspoon vanilla extract

1. In a small saucepan over low heat, combine all ingredients. Cook, stirring, until smooth.
2. Increase heat. Boil 2 to 3 minutes or until slightly reduced. Serve hot or cover and refrigerate until chilled. Makes about 1 cup.

To Make Chocolate Sauces

1. For a smooth chocolate sauce, stir constantly while cooking. If lumps form, beat with a whisk.
2. If a sauce contains cocoa, cook to eliminate any starchy taste. For a quick sauce that needs no cooking, use a chocolate-flavored drink mix. Drink mixes are already sweetened; sweeten to taste using corn syrup or honey.
3. Most chocolate sauces thicken when cooled. Thin with a little milk, cream or a liqueur, such as Tia Maria.

Soufflé Monte Carlo

1 tablespoon instant coffee powder
1 tablespoon boiling water
1 (1/4-oz.) envelope unflavored gelatin (1 tablespoon)
1/2 cup granulated sugar
4 eggs, separated
1/2 cup cold water
1-3/4 cups whipping cream
3 tablespoons powdered sugar
1 cup almond-macaroon crumbs
1/4 cup coffee-flavored liqueur
4 oz. semisweet chocolate, finely chopped
Chocolate coffee-bean candies

To decorate:
Chocolate scrolls, page 8

1. Wrap a 3-inch foil collar around outside of a 1-quart glass soufflé dish. Secure collar with a small piece of tape.
2. In a small bowl, dissolve coffee in boiling water. Combine gelatin and granulated sugar in top of a double boiler. Whisk egg yolks and cold water into dissolved coffee until blended. Whisk egg mixture into gelatin mixture until blended.
3. Place over a pan of simmering water. Cook, stirring constantly, until mixture thickens and coats back of a spoon. Pour cooked coffee mixture into a large bowl. Let cool 15 minutes, stirring occasionally. Cover surface with a sheet of waxed paper to prevent a skin from forming; refrigerate until cooled.
4. In a medium bowl, beat cream until soft peaks form. Beat in powdered sugar. Spoon 2/3 cup whipped-cream mixture into a pastry bag fitted with a star or rosette tip; refrigerate. Fold remaining whipped-cream mixture into cooled coffee mixture. Refrigerate 30 minutes.
5. In a small bowl, combine cookie crumbs and liqueur; let stand until liqueur is absorbed. Stir in chocolate.
6. In a large bowl, beat egg whites until stiff but not dry. Fold beaten egg whites into chilled coffee cream.
7. Sprinkle a layer of crumb mixture into bottom of prepared soufflé dish. Top with a layer of coffee cream. Repeat to make 3 layers of each, ending with coffee cream. Refrigerate 3 hours or until set.
8. Carefully remove foil collar from soufflé dish. Pipe reserved whipped-cream mixture in rosettes on top of soufflé. Decorate with coffee-bean candies and chocolate scrolls. Refrigerate until served. Makes 6 to 8 servings.

Chocolate-Mint Soufflé

2 tablespoons sugar
1/4 cup butter or margarine
1/4 cup all-purpose flour
1 cup milk
1/4 cup sugar
3 oz. semisweet or sweet chocolate, chopped
4 egg yolks
2 tablespoons white or green crème de menthe
5 egg whites

Sauce:
2/3 cup whipping cream
2 oz. semisweet chocolate, chopped
1 egg yolk, beaten
2 tablespoons white or green crème de menthe

1. Butter a 1-1/2-quart 7-inch soufflé dish. Sprinkle with about 2 tablespoons sugar; shake out excess.
2. Melt butter or margarine in a medium saucepan over medium heat. Whisk in flour to make a smooth roux. Cook, stirring, 1 minute. Gradually whisk in milk; cook, stirring constantly, until mixture thickens and comes to a boil. Whisk in 1/4 cup sugar. Add chocolate; stir until chocolate melts. Remove from heat.
3. In a small bowl, slightly beat egg yolks. Stir 1/4 cup hot sauce into egg yolks until blended. Return mixture to saucepan; stir well. Cook, stirring, until thickened. Do not boil. Pour into a large bowl; stir in crème de menthe. Cover surface with a sheet of waxed paper to prevent a skin from forming; refrigerate until cooled.
4. Preheat oven to 350F (175C). In a large bowl, beat egg whites until stiff but not dry. Fold beaten egg whites into cooled chocolate mixture. Pour mixture into prepared dish.
5. Bake in preheated oven 40 to 50 minutes or until puffed and a skewer inserted in center comes out clean.
6. While soufflé is baking, make sauce. To make sauce, in a small saucepan over low heat, combine cream and chocolate. Cook, stirring, until chocolate melts and mixture is smooth. Remove from heat. Whisk in egg yolk and crème de menthe until smooth. Pour into a small serving pitcher.
7. Remove soufflé from oven; serve immediately with sauce. Makes 6 servings.

Left to right: Soufflé Monte Carlo, Chocolate-Mint Soufflé

Ginger Charlotte Russe

Topping:
1 teaspoon unflavored gelatin powder
5 tablespoons water
5 tablespoons ginger wine or ginger brandy
1/2 maraschino cherry
5 candied orange slices or 5 canned mandarin-orange
    sections, drained
1 thin strip angelica, about 2 inches long
About 8 whole ladyfingers, split lengthwise

Bavarian:
1 (1/4-oz.) envelope unflavored gelatin (1 tablespoon)
1/3 cup granulated sugar
1 cup milk
2 oz. semisweet chocolate, chopped
2 eggs, separated
1/4 cup ginger wine or ginger brandy
1-1/4 cups whipping cream
2 tablespoons powdered sugar

To decorate:
1 (3-foot) ribbon, if desired

Left to right: Ginger Charlotte Russe, Chocolate-Pear Cake,
Mandarin-Yogurt Dessert

1. To make topping, in a small saucepan, combine gelatin and water. Stir well; let stand 3 minutes. Stir over low heat until gelatin dissolves; cool slightly. Stir in wine or brandy.
2. Pour half of gelatin mixture into bottom of a 2-quart, 6-inch-diameter charlotte mold. Place cherry, rounded-side down, in bottom of mold. Arrange candied orange slices or orange sections around cherry to resemble a flower. Use strip of angelica for stem. Refrigerate 30 minutes or until gelatin is firm.
3. Pour remaining dissolved gelatin mixture into mold; refrigerate 10 to 15 minutes or until almost set. Line mold with ladyfingers, pushing bottom ends of ladyfingers into almost-set gelatin. Refrigerate until gelatin is firm.
4. To make bavarian, in a medium saucepan, combine gelatin and granulated sugar. Stir in milk. Cook over low heat, stirring, until gelatin dissolves. Stir in chocolate; cook until mixture thickens and coats back of a spoon. Remove pan from heat.
5. In a small bowl, slightly beat egg yolks. Stir 1/4 cup hot chocolate mixture into beaten egg yolks until blended. Return mixture to saucepan; stir well. Cook, stirring, until mixture is thickened. Do not boil.
6. Pour into a medium bowl. Stir in wine or brandy. Cover surface with a sheet of waxed paper to prevent a skin from forming. Refrigerate until mixture mounds when dropped from a spoon.
7. In a medium bowl, beat cream until soft peaks form. Beat in powdered sugar. Spoon 1/3 of whipped-cream mixture into a pastry bag fitted with a star or rosette tip; refrigerate. Fold remaining whipped-cream mixture into chilled chocolate mixture.

8. In a medium bowl, beat egg whites until stiff but not dry. Fold beaten egg whites into chocolate-cream mixture. Spoon mixture into lined charlotte mold; smooth top. Refrigerate several hours or until set.
9. To unmold, dip bottom of mold into hot water; invert onto a serving plate. Remove mold. Pipe chilled whipped-cream mixture in small rosettes on top of each ladyfinger. Refrigerate until served. Tie with ribbon immediately before serving, if desired. Makes 6 to 8 servings.

3. In a medium bowl, combine cooled gelatin mixture and yogurt. Gradually stir in melted chocolate until blended. Stir in reserved chopped orange sections, grated chocolate and liqueur until combined.

4. Pour mixture into a 2-1/2-cup decorative mold. Refrigerate 2 to 3 hours or until set.

5. To unmold, run tip of a knife around edge of mold to loosen. Rinse a towel under hot running water; wring dry. Wrap hot towel around mold; let stand 1 minute. Invert mold onto a serving plate; remove mold.

6. To serve, in a small bowl, beat cream until soft peaks form. Beat in powdered sugar. Spoon whipped-cream mixture into a pastry bag fitted with a star or rosette tip. Pipe a large rosette in center of molded mixture. Pipe small rosettes around base. Decorate top with reserved orange section and chocolate leaf. Refrigerate until served. Makes 6 servings.

Chocolate-Pear Cake

Topping:
1/4 cup butter or margarine
1/3 cup firmly packed dark-brown sugar
1 (29-oz.) can pear halves, well drained
6 maraschino cherries or red candied cherries

Cake:
1/3 cup butter or margarine, room temperature
3/4 cup sugar
2 eggs
1 cup all-purpose flour
1/4 cup unsweetened cocoa powder
1 teaspoon baking powder
1/2 teaspoon salt
1/3 cup milk

To decorate:
Sliced almonds, if desired

1. Preheat oven to 350F (175C). Place butter or margarine in a deep 8-inch-round cake pan. Melt butter or margarine in preheated oven. Remove from oven. Sprinkle brown sugar over melted butter or margarine. Arrange 6 pear halves, cut-side down, on top of sugar. Slide 1 cherry under cavity of each pear half. Chop remaining pears; set aside.

2. To make cake, in a medium bowl, beat butter or margarine, sugar, eggs, flour, cocoa, baking powder, salt and milk with an electric mixer at low speed 1 minute or until blended.

3. Increase speed to medium; beat 2 minutes, scraping down side of bowl occasionally. Fold in reserved chopped pears. Carefully spoon batter over pear halves; smooth top.

4. Bake in preheated oven 45 to 50 minutes or until a wooden pick inserted in center comes out clean. Cool in pan on wire rack 2 minutes. Invert onto a serving plate; leave pan in place 3 minutes. Carefully remove pan. Serve warm or at room temperature. Decorate with sliced almonds, if desired. Makes 6 to 8 servings.

Mandarin-Yogurt Dessert

1 (11-oz.) can mandarin-orange sections
1 (1/4-oz.) envelope unflavored gelatin (1 tablespoon)
8 oz. plain yogurt or vanilla-flavored yogurt (1 cup)
3 oz. semisweet chocolate, melted, cooled
1 oz. semisweet chocolate, finely grated
2 tablespoons orange-flavored liqueur
1/2 cup whipping cream
1 tablespoon powdered sugar

To decorate:
Chocolate leaf, page 7

1. Drain oranges, reserving syrup. Set 1 orange section aside for decoration. Coarsely chop remaining orange sections; set aside.

2. In a small saucepan, combine gelatin and reserved orange syrup. Stir well; let stand 3 minutes. Stir over low heat until gelatin dissolves; set aside to cool.

Banana Bavarian

1 (3-oz.) pkg. lemon-flavored gelatin
1 cup boiling water
2 small bananas
1/4 cup granulated sugar
1 (1/4-oz.) envelope unflavored gelatin (1 tablespoon)
1-1/4 cups milk
3 eggs, separated
1 teaspoon grated lemon peel
1 teaspoon vanilla extract
1/2 pint whipping cream (1 cup)
2 tablespoons powdered sugar
4 oz. semisweet or bittersweet chocolate, coarsely
    chopped

1. In a medium bowl, dissolve lemon gelatin in boiling water. Pour 1/2 cup gelatin into bottom of an 8" x 4" loaf pan. Refrigerate 30 minutes or until firm. Thinly slice bananas; add to remaining lemon gelatin, stirring gently until banana slices are coated.

2. Remove banana slices with a slotted spoon; arrange in 3 lengthwise rows over set gelatin, slightly overlapping slices. Repeat with remaining banana slices. Spoon remaining lemon gelatin over banana slices; refrigerate until firm.

3. In a medium saucepan, combine granulated sugar and unflavored gelatin; stir in milk until smooth. Cook over low heat, stirring, until mixture thickens and coats back of a spoon. Remove from heat.

4. In a small bowl, slightly beat egg yolks. Stir 1/4 cup hot milk mixture into beaten egg yolks until blended. Return mixture to saucepan; stir well. Cook, stirring, until thickened. Do not boil. Pour into a large bowl.

5. Stir in lemon peel and vanilla until blended. Cover surface of custard with a sheet of waxed paper to prevent a skin from forming. Refrigerate about 45 minutes or until mixture mounds when dropped from a spoon.

6. In a medium bowl, beat cream until soft peaks form. Beat in powdered sugar. Fold 1/2 of whipped-cream mixture into chilled custard. Refrigerate remaining whipped-cream mixture.

7. In a medium bowl, beat egg whites until stiff but not dry. Fold beaten egg whites into custard mixture. Spoon custard-egg-white mixture over banana layer; smooth top. Refrigerate 3 to 4 hours or until set.

Left to right: Banana Bavarian, Steamed Fudge Pudding

8. Run tip of a knife around edge of pan to loosen dessert. Dip pan into hot water 30 seconds. Invert onto a serving plate; carefully remove pan.

9. Spread 1/2 of reserved whipped-cream mixture around sides of bavarian, smoothing cream with a long spatula. Spoon remaining reserved whipped-cream mixture into a pastry bag fitted with a small open-star tip; refrigerate.

10. Melt chocolate in a small heavy saucepan over very low heat; stir until smooth. Cool slightly. Spread chocolate on a sheet of foil to a 12" x 8" rectangle. Let stand until chocolate is set. Cut chocolate into 2" x 1" rectangles. Arrange chocolate rectangles lengthwise, slightly overlapping, around sides of bavarian, pressing rectangles gently into whipped cream. Pipe chilled whipped-cream mixture decoratively around top edge of chocolate rectangles. Refrigerate until served. Makes 8 to 10 servings.

Steamed Fudge Pudding

Pudding:
1/4 cup butter or margarine, room temperature
3/4 cup sugar
1 egg
1 cup self-rising flour
1/4 cup unsweetened cocoa powder
1/4 cup milk

Custard Sauce:
1 tablespoon cornstarch
1/3 cup sugar
1/4 teaspoon salt
2 cups milk
3 egg yolks, beaten
1 teaspoon vanilla extract

To decorate:
Grated chocolate, if desired

1. Grease a 1-quart heatproof bowl or pudding mold. Cut a double thickness of foil large enough to cover top of bowl or mold and extend 2 inches down sides; grease 1 side.

2. To make pudding, in a medium bowl, beat butter or margarine and sugar until light and fluffy. Beat in egg until blended. Sift flour and cocoa into a medium bowl. Add flour mixture to sugar mixture alternately with milk; beat until blended.

3. Spoon into greased bowl or mold; smooth top. Cover bowl with foil, greased-side down; secure with kitchen string.

4. Place bowl or mold on a rack in a large deep pan. Pour in enough boiling water to come two-thirds of way up side of bowl or mold. Cover pan; steam pudding 1-1/4 to 1-1/2 hours or until a wooden pick inserted in center of pudding comes out clean, adding more boiling water as necessary to maintain water level. Remove pudding from pan; uncover. Let stand 5 minutes. Invert pudding onto a serving dish; remove bowl or mold.

5. To make custard sauce, in top of a double boiler, combine cornstarch, sugar and salt. Gradually stir in milk until smooth. Cook over a pan of simmering water, stirring, until sugar dissolves and mixture is slightly thickened. Remove from heat. Stir 6 tablespoons hot milk mixture into beaten egg yolks until thoroughly blended. Return mixture to pan; stir well. Cook, stirring, until mixture thickens and coats back of a spoon. Remove from heat; stir in vanilla.

6. Serve sauce warm or refrigerate until cooled. To serve, pour 1/2 of sauce over pudding; serve remaining sauce separately. Sprinkle pudding with chocolate, if desired. Makes 4 to 6 servings.

Apricot & Chocolate Cheesecake

1 (11-1/2-oz.) pkg. creme-filled chocolate rolls (8 small rolls)
1 (1-lb.) can apricot halves
2 (8-oz.) pkgs. cream cheese, room temperature
1/3 cup granulated sugar
1 tablespoon lemon juice
2 eggs, separated
1 (1/4-oz.) envelope unflavored gelatin (1 tablespoon)
1/2 cup whipping cream
1 tablespoon powdered sugar

To decorate:
1 oz. semisweet chocolate, chopped
1 teaspoon vegetable shortening

---

1. Cut rolls into 1/2-inch-thick slices; use slices to line side and bottom of a 10-inch serving dish or glass pie dish.
2. Drain apricots, reserving 1/4 cup syrup. Set 4 apricots aside for decoration. In a blender or food processor fitted with a steel blade, process remaining apricots until pureed.
3. In a large bowl, beat cream cheese, granulated sugar and lemon juice until fluffy. Beat in egg yolks until blended. Beat in pureed apricots until blended.
4. In a small saucepan, combine gelatin and reserved apricot syrup. Stir well; let stand 3 minutes. Stir over low heat until gelatin dissolves; let cool.
5. Stir cooled gelatin mixture into cream-cheese mixture. Refrigerate about 30 minutes or until mixture is thickened.
6. In a medium bowl, beat cream until soft peaks form. Beat in powdered sugar. Fold 1/2 of whipped-cream mixture into cream-cheese mixture. Spoon remaining whipped-cream mixture into a pastry bag fitted with a star or rosette tip; refrigerate.
7. In a medium bowl, beat egg whites until stiff but not dry. Fold beaten egg whites into cream-cheese mixture. Pour cream-cheese mixture into cake-lined dish; smooth top. Refrigerate several hours or until set.
8. To decorate, in a small saucepan over low heat, melt chocolate and shortening; stir until smooth. Remove from heat; let cool. Spoon chocolate into a pastry bag fitted with a small plain writing tip. Pipe chocolate in parallel lines about 1 inch apart on top of cheesecake. Draw point of a sharp knife across piped lines in alternate directions to create a feathered effect.
9. Pipe chilled whipped-cream mixture in small rosettes around edge of cheesecake. Cut reserved apricots in half. Cut each apricot half into a fan shape; place between rosettes. Refrigerate until served. Makes 8 to 10 servings.

Chocolate Chiffon Pie

Pastry:
1-1/2 cups all-purpose flour
2 tablespoons sugar
1/4 teaspoon salt
1/2 cup butter or margarine
1 egg yolk
2 to 2-1/2 tablespoons iced water

Filling:
1/2 cup half and half
1/2 cup sugar
1 (1/4-oz.) envelope unflavored gelatin (1 tablespoon)
1/2 cup water
2 eggs, separated
2 oz. unsweetened chocolate, chopped

To decorate:
Powdered sugar
2 oz. semisweet or sweet chocolate, finely grated

---

1. Preheat oven to 425F (220C). To make pastry, in a medium bowl, combine flour, sugar and salt. With a pastry blender or 2 knives, cut in butter or margarine until mixture resembles coarse crumbs. In a small bowl, beat egg yolk and 2 tablespoons water until blended. Sprinkle over flour; toss with a fork until mixture binds together, adding additional water if necessary. Knead dough in bowl 8 to 10 strokes or until smooth.
2. On a lightly floured surface, roll out pastry to an 11-inch circle. Use pastry to line a 9-inch quiche pan or tart pan with a removable bottom. Trim pastry even with rim of pan. Prick bottom of pastry with a fork. Line pastry with foil; fill with pie weights or dried beans.
3. Bake in preheated oven 10 minutes. Remove foil and pie weights or beans; reduce oven temperature to 375F (190C). Bake 5 to 8 minutes or until golden. Cool completely in pan on a wire rack.
4. To make filling, in a medium saucepan, whisk half and half, sugar, gelatin, water and egg yolks until thoroughly blended. Stir in chocolate. Cook over low heat, stirring constantly, until chocolate melts and gelatin dissolves. Pour into a medium bowl.
5. Beat chocolate mixture with an electric mixer at high speed 1 minute. Refrigerate 45 minutes or until thickened.
6. In a medium bowl, beat egg whites until stiff but not dry. Beat chocolate mixture on high speed 2 minutes or until fluffy. Fold beaten egg whites into beaten chocolate mixture. Pour into cooled pastry shell; smooth top. Refrigerate 2 to 3 hours or until set.
7. To serve, remove pie from pan; place on a serving plate. Sift powdered sugar over top; top with rows of chocolate. Makes 6 to 8 servings.

Left to right: Chocolate Chiffon Pie, Apricot & Chocolate Cheesecake, Hot Chocolate Trifle

Hot Chocolate Trifle

1 (11-1/2-oz.) pkg. jelly-filled rolls (8 small rolls)
1/4 cup sweet sherry
2 eggs
1 egg yolk
1/3 cup sugar
1 teaspoon vanilla extract
1-1/4 cups milk, scalded
2 oz. semisweet chocolate, melted

To decorate:
1/4 cup chopped red candied cherries
1/4 cup chopped walnuts, pecans or almonds

1. Grease a 1-quart ovenproof serving bowl. Cut rolls into 1/2-inch-thick slices; use slices to line bottom and side of bowl. Cut remaining jelly-roll slices into cubes. Add cubed jelly-roll slices to bowl. Sprinkle sherry over cake; set aside.
2. In a medium bowl, beat eggs, egg yolk, sugar and vanilla until blended. Gradually beat in hot milk and chocolate until combined. Pour custard through a fine sieve over cake in bowl. Let stand 30 minutes.
3. Preheat oven to 350F (175C). Place bowl in a deep pan. Pour in enough boiling water to come halfway up side of bowl.
4. Bake in preheated oven 1 hour 15 minutes or until custard is set. Remove bowl from pan; cool slightly on a wire rack.
5. Sprinkle with cherries and nuts immediately before serving. Serve warm or refrigerate until chilled. Makes 6 servings.

Chocolate-Pecan Pots

1/2 cup pecan halves
1 (8-oz.) pkg. cream cheese, room temperature
1 tablespoon milk
1 tablespoon honey
2 teaspoons grated lemon peel
1 tablespoon lemon juice
1/3 cup chopped pitted dates
4 oz. semisweet chocolate
1 tablespoon butter or margarine

1. Set 4 pecan halves aside for decoration. Chop remaining pecans.

2. In a medium bowl, beat cream cheese until fluffy. Beat in milk, honey, lemon peel and lemon juice until blended. Fold in chopped pecans and dates.

3. Grate 2 ounces chocolate; fold into cream-cheese mixture. Spoon chocolate mixture into 4 (1/2-cup) ramekins; smooth tops.

4. Melt remaining 2 ounces chocolate and butter or margarine in a small saucepan over low heat; stir until smooth. Cool slightly.

5. Spoon a little melted chocolate over top of each dish; spread evenly. Place a reserved pecan half in center of each dish. Refrigerate 1 hour or until served. Makes 4 servings.

Strawberry-Cheesecake Boxes

Chocolate Mousse

5 oz. semisweet chocolate, coarsely chopped
2 tablespoons strong black coffee
4 eggs, separated
1 tablespoon orange-flavored liqueur
1/2 pint whipping cream (1 cup)
2 tablespoons powdered sugar
Shaved chocolate, page 7

1. Melt chocolate in a medium heavy saucepan over very low heat; stir until smooth. Stir in coffee until blended. Remove from heat.
2. In a small bowl, slightly beat egg yolks. Stir in 3 tablespoons chocolate mixture until blended. Return mixture to pan.
3. Cook over low heat, stirring, 1 minute. Pour chocolate mixture into a medium bowl. Stir in liqueur; refrigerate until cool.
4. In a medium bowl, beat cream until soft peaks form. Beat in powdered sugar. Reserve 3/4 cup whipped-cream mixture for decoration; cover and refrigerate. Fold remaining whipped-cream mixture into cooled chocolate mixture.
5. In a medium bowl, beat egg whites until stiff but not dry. Fold beaten egg whites into chocolate-cream mixture. Spoon mixture into 6 to 8 individual ramekins, champagne glasses or a large serving bowl. Refrigerate at least 3 hours or overnight. To serve, spoon a dollop of reserved whipped-cream mixture on top of each serving; sprinkle with shaved chocolate. Makes 6 to 8 servings.

Strawberry-Cheesecake Boxes

Cake:
2 eggs
1/3 cup sugar
1/2 teaspoon vanilla extract
1/2 cup sifted cake flour

Filling:
1 (3-oz.) pkg. strawberry-flavored gelatin
1/2 teaspoon unflavored gelatin powder
1 cup boiling water
1 tablespoon lemon juice
1 (8-oz.) pkg. cream cheese, room temperature
1/2 pint whipping cream (1 cup)
2 tablespoons powdered sugar
4 to 5 tablespoons red-currant jelly, melted, cooled

To decorate:
10 oz. semisweet or sweet chocolate, chopped
8 fresh strawberries, washed, hulled

1. Preheat oven to 375F (190C). Grease an 8-inch-square baking pan. Line bottom of pan with waxed paper; grease paper.
2. To make cake, in a medium bowl, beat eggs and sugar 10 to 12 minutes or until thick and lemon-colored. Mixture should fall in thick ribbons when beaters are lifted. Beat in vanilla.
3. Sift flour over egg mixture; fold in. Pour batter into prepared pan; smooth top.
4. Bake in preheated oven 18 to 20 minutes or until center springs back when lightly pressed. Cool in pan on a wire rack 5 minutes. Remove from pan; peel off lining paper. Cool completely on wire rack.
5. To make filling, line an 8-inch-square pan with waxed paper. In a small bowl, combine strawberry-flavored gelatin and unflavored gelatin. Stir in boiling water until gelatins dissolve. Stir in lemon juice. Refrigerate 30 to 40 minutes or until gelatin is syrupy.
6. In a large bowl, beat cream cheese until fluffy. Gradually beat in chilled gelatin mixture until blended. Refrigerate 30 minutes or until thickened.
7. In a medium bowl, beat cream until soft peaks form. Beat in powdered sugar. Spoon about 2/3 cup whipped-cream mixture into a pastry bag fitted with a star or rosette tip; refrigerate. Fold remaining whipped-cream mixture into cream-cheese mixture. Pour mixture into prepared pan. Refrigerate 3 hours or until set.
8. Place cooled cake on a flat surface; brush top lightly with jelly. Invert strawberry cheesecake on top of cake; peel off paper. Trim filling even with cake edges, if necessary. Cut into 16 (2-inch) squares.
9. To decorate, tape 2 waxed-paper or parchment-paper pieces together, making an area larger than a 16-inch square. Draw a 16-inch square on paper. Melt chocolate in a small heavy saucepan over very low heat; stir until smooth. Let cool slightly. Spread melted chocolate inside square. When chocolate is almost set, with a sharp knife, score into 64 (2-inch) squares. Let stand until completely set. Cut chocolate with a sharp knife along scored lines.
10. Brush sides of each cheesecake-topped cake square lightly with jelly. Press 4 chocolate squares onto sides of each cake square.
11. Pipe chilled whipped-cream mixture in a rosette in center of each square. Cut strawberries in half; place a strawberry half on each rosette. Place on a serving plate; refrigerate until served or up to 4 hours. Makes 16 servings.

Chocolate Bread Pudding

2 tablespoons butter or margarine, room temperature
5 white-bread slices, crusts removed
1 teaspoon ground cinnamon
2-1/4 cups milk
1 teaspoon instant coffee powder
2 oz. semisweet chocolate, chopped
3 eggs
1/3 cup sugar
1 oz. semisweet chocolate, grated

1. Grease a 1-1/2- to 2-quart casserole.
2. Spread butter or margarine on 1 side of bread slices; sprinkle with cinnamon. Cut slices into 4 triangles; place triangles in greased casserole.
3. In a medium saucepan over low heat, combine milk, coffee and chopped chocolate. Cook, stirring, until chocolate melts. Remove from heat.
4. In a medium bowl, beat eggs and sugar until thick and lemon-colored.
5. Pour hot milk mixture into egg mixture in a slow steady stream, beating constantly. Pour milk mixture over bread in casserole; let stand at room temperature 30 minutes. perature 30 minutes.
6. Preheat oven to 350F (175C). Place casserole in a deep roasting pan; pour in enough boiling water to come halfway up side of casserole.
7. Bake in preheated oven 1 hour. Sprinkle grated chocolate over top of pudding; bake 10 minutes or until pudding is set. Serve warm or chilled. Makes 4 to 6 servings.

Crowning Glory

8 oz. semisweet chocolate, coarsely chopped
1/4 cup butter or margarine
2 eggs
3 tablespoons dark rum
1-2/3 cups vanilla-wafer or chocolate-cookie crumbs
   (35 to 40 cookies)
1/3 cup chopped toasted hazelnuts or almonds
1/3 cup red candied cherries, quartered
1/2 cup whipping cream
1 tablespoon powdered sugar
6 maraschino cherries

Serve this rich confection in small slices. This is a good summertime dessert; no baking is required!

1. Generously grease a 3-cup ring mold. Melt chocolate and butter or margarine in a medium heavy saucepan over very low heat. Stir until smooth.
2. In a medium bowl, beat eggs until blended. Whisk in 4 to 5 tablespoons melted chocolate mixture. Beat in remaining chocolate mixture until blended.
3. Beat in rum until blended. Stir in cookie crumbs, nuts and candied cherries until combined. Pour into greased mold; smooth top. Refrigerate 3 hours or until firm.
4. In a medium bowl, beat cream until soft peaks form. Beat in powdered sugar. Spoon whipped-cream mixture into a pastry bag fitted with a medium rosette or star tip; refrigerate.
5. To serve, dip mold in hot water 20 seconds. Invert onto a serving plate. Remove mold. Pipe 6 whipped-cream rosettes on top of mold; decorate with maraschino cherries. Refrigerate until served. Makes 6 to 8 servings.

Rum & Raisin Mousse

1/3 cup raisins
1/4 cup rum
4 oz. semisweet chocolate, broken into pieces
2 eggs, separated
1-1/4 cups whipping cream

1. In a small bowl, combine raisins and rum. Cover and let stand 8 hours or overnight.
2. Melt chocolate in a small saucepan over very low heat; stir until smooth. Cool slightly.
3. Beat in egg yolks. Stir in raisins and rum.
4. In a medium bowl, beat cream until almost stiff. Spoon 1/2 cup whipped cream into a pastry bag fitted with a star or rosette tip; refrigerate. Fold remaining whipped cream into chocolate mixture.
5. In a medium bowl, beat egg whites until stiff but not dry. Fold beaten egg whites into chocolate mixture.
6. Spoon mixture into a 2-cup freezer-to-table serving dish; freeze about 2 hours or until barely firm. If frozen firm, soften in refrigerator before serving.
7. Pipe chilled whipped cream in a shell border around edge of mousse. Makes 4 servings.

Left to right: Rum & Raisin Mousse, Chocolate Bread Pudding, Chocolate Hearts

Chocolate Hearts

3 oz. semisweet chocolate, chopped
1 (8-oz.) pkg. cream cheese, room temperature
2 tablespoons granulated sugar
2 teaspoons grated orange peel
1/3 cup orange juice
1 teaspoon unflavored gelatin powder
1/2 cup whipping cream
1 teaspoon powdered sugar

To serve:
1 recipe Quick Chocolate Sauce, page 21, or sweetened
   whipped cream
Small chocolate hearts, page 8
Fresh orange sections

1. Dampen 4 pieces of double cheesecloth large enough to line 4 individual coeur a la crème molds or heart-shaped molds. Line molds with damp cheesecloth. Melt chocolate in a small heavy saucepan over very low heat; stir until smooth. Let cool slightly.
2. In a medium bowl, beat cream cheese and granulated sugar until fluffy. Beat in orange peel. Gradually beat in cooled chocolate.
3. In a small saucepan, combine orange juice and gelatin. Stir well; let stand 3 minutes. Stir over low heat until gelatin dissolves; let cool.
4. Stir cooled gelatin into chocolate mixture until thoroughly blended. Refrigerate 20 minutes or until thickened.
5. In a medium bowl, beat cream until soft peaks form. Beat in powdered sugar. Fold whipped-cream mixture into chocolate mixture.
6. Spoon chocolate mixture into lined molds; smooth tops. Fold ends of cheesecloth over top of chocolate mixture. Place mold in a baking pan. Refrigerate 2 hours.
7. Unfold ends of cheesecloth; invert molds onto 4 serving plates. Remove cheesecloth. Spread each heart with a thin layer of chocolate sauce, or decorate with sweetened whipped cream and chocolate hearts. Serve with fresh orange sections. Makes 4 servings.

Cream Puffs with Chocolate Sauce

Choux Paste:
1/2 cup butter or margarine
1 cup water
1 tablespoon sugar
1/4 teaspoon salt
1 cup sifted all-purpose flour
4 eggs

Filling:
2 tablespoons cornstarch
6 tablespoons granulated sugar
1 tablespoon unsweetened cocoa powder
1 cup milk
3 egg yolks, beaten
3/4 cup whipping cream
1 teaspoon vanilla extract
2 tablespoons powdered sugar

To serve:
1 recipe Special Chocolate Sauce, page 21

1. Preheat oven to 400F (205C). Grease 2 baking sheets.
2. To make choux paste, in a medium saucepan over medium heat, combine butter or margarine, water, sugar and salt; bring to a boil. Stir in flour, all at once, with a wooden spoon until dough forms a ball and comes away from side of pan. Cool slightly.
3. Beat in eggs, 1 at a time, beating well after each addition.
4. Spoon dough into a pastry bag fitted with a large plain tip. Pipe 24 small balls about 2 inches apart on greased baking sheets.
5. Bake in preheated oven 25 to 30 minutes or until puffed and golden brown. Remove from baking sheets; cut a small slit in side of each cream puff to let steam escape. Cool completely on wire racks.
6. To make filling, in a medium saucepan, combine cornstarch, granulated sugar and cocoa. Stir in milk until blended. Cook, stirring, until mixture thickens and comes to a boil. Remove from heat. Stir 1/4 cup hot mixture into egg yolks until blended. Return mixture to saucepan; stir well. Cook, stirring, until mixture thickens. Do not boil.
7. Pour custard into a large bowl. Cover surface with a sheet of waxed paper to prevent a skin from forming. Refrigerate 2 to 3 hours or until completely chilled.
8. In a medium bowl, beat cream until soft peaks form. Beat in vanilla and powdered sugar. Fold whipped-cream mixture into chilled custard.
9. Cut tops off cream puffs. Remove and discard any soft dough from insides. Spoon filling into a pastry bag fitted with a large plain tip; pipe filling into bottom half of cream puffs. Replace tops.
10. Place filled cream puffs on a serving plate. Pour a little chocolate sauce over cream puffs; serve remaining sauce separately. Makes 24 cream puffs.

Chocolate & Almond Pastry

1-1/2 cups sponge-cake crumbs
2/3 cup finely chopped almonds
1/4 cup granulated sugar
1/3 cup unsweetened cocoa powder
1/4 cup prepared mincemeat
1/3 cup butter or margarine, room temperature
1 egg, beaten
1/2 (17-1/4-oz. pkg.) frozen puff pastry, thawed (1 sheet)
About 3 tablespoons milk
About 2 tablespoons powdered sugar

1. Preheat oven to 425F (220C).
2. In a medium bowl, combine cake crumbs, almonds, granulated sugar, cocoa, mincemeat, butter or margarine and egg. Beat with a wooden spoon until thoroughly blended; set aside.
3. On a lightly floured surface, unfold pastry. Roll out pastry to a 13" x 11" rectangle. Place on an ungreased baking sheet. With a blunt knife, score 2 straight lines lengthwise 3 inches in from each long side of pastry.
4. Spread chocolate-crumb mixture in a 4-inch-wide strip lengthwise down center of pastry between scored lines to within 1/2 inch of lines.
5. Cut pastry diagonally at 1/2-inch intervals on sides of filling from scored lines to edge of pastry. Brush pastry strips lightly with milk. Fold ends of pastry over filling. Alternately fold pastry strips over filling overlapping strips in center. Brush pastry with milk; sprinkle with powdered sugar.
6. Bake in preheated oven 25 to 30 minutes or until pastry is puffed and golden brown. Remove from baking sheet; cool completely on a wire rack. Slice to serve. Makes 8 to 10 servings.

Left to right: Cream Puffs with Chocolate Sauce, Chocolate & Almond Pastry

Windmill Cake

1/2 recipe (1 layer), Cocoa Layer Cake, page 51
1/2 recipe (1 layer), Sponge Layers, page 43
1/3 cup seedless raspberry jam, melted, cooled

Frosting:
1 cup butter or margarine, room temperature
1 (16-oz.) box powdered sugar, sifted
2 tablespoons half and half
2 teaspoons peppermint extract
2 tablespoons unsweetened cocoa powder
2 tablespoons boiling water

1. Prepare and bake cake layers as directed on pages 51 and 43, using 8-inch-round pans. Cool layers in pans on wire racks 5 minutes. Remove from pans; cool completely on wire racks.
2. Cut 2 cardboard circles, 1 (2-inch) circle and 1 (5-inch) circle.
3. Place 5-inch circle in center of cocoa layer; cut around circle. Remove cardboard circle. Place 2-inch circle in center of cocoa layer; cut around circle. Remove cardboard circle. Remove both cake circles carefully. Set aside. Repeat with sponge layer.
4. Brush cut edges of cake circles with raspberry jam. Reassemble both cake layers, alternating cocoa and sponge circles to match photo.
5. To make frosting, in a large bowl, beat butter or margarine until creamy. Add 2-1/4 cups powdered sugar; beat until light and fluffy. Beat in remaining powdered sugar and half and half. Beat until frosting is fluffy and a good consistency for spreading. Spoon 1/3 of frosting into a medium bowl.
6. Beat peppermint extract into medium bowl of frosting. In a small bowl, blend cocoa and boiling water; cool slightly. Beat cooled cocoa mixture into large bowl of frosting.
7. Place 1 cake layer on a serving plate; spread with 1/3 of chocolate frosting. Top with second layer. Spoon remaining frostings into separate pastry bags fitted with small open-star tips. Score cake into 8 equal wedges. Pipe stars of peppermint frosting on 4 alternate wedges, covering wedges completely. Pipe stars of chocolate frosting on remaining wedges. Let stand until frosting is set. Makes 8 servings.

Chocolate-Filled Meringue Layers

Meringue Layers:
6 egg whites
1/4 teaspoon cream of tartar
1-1/2 cups superfine sugar
1 teaspoon vanilla extract

Filling:
1 teaspoon instant coffee powder
1 tablespoon boiling water
2 tablespoons dark rum or brandy
3/4 cup finely chopped, toasted, blanched almonds
1/2 recipe warm Ganache Crème, page 38
1/2 pint whipping cream (1 cup)
1 tablespoon powdered sugar
Chocolate curls, page 7

1. Preheat oven to 200F (95C). Line 2 large baking sheets with parchment paper. Draw 3 (9-inch) circles on parchment paper.
2. In a large bowl, with an electric mixer at high speed, beat egg whites and cream of tartar until soft peaks form. Gradually beat in superfine sugar, beating constantly until meringue is stiff and glossy. Beat in vanilla. Spread meringue inside circles on lined baking sheets.
3. Bake in preheated oven 2 hours or until meringues are crisp and dry. Remove from oven; cool on baking sheets on wire racks. When cool, carefully peel off lining paper.
4. To make filling, dissolve coffee in boiling water. Beat dissolved coffee, rum or brandy and almonds into Ganache Crème until blended. Cover and refrigerate 4 hours.
5. Beat chilled ganache mixture with a heavy-duty mixer until soft. In a medium bowl, beat whipping cream until soft peaks form. Beat in powdered sugar. Beat 1/2 of whipped-cream mixture into softened ganache mixture. Reserve remaining whipped-cream mixture.
6. Place 1 meringue layer on a serving plate; spread with 1/2 of ganache mixture. Top with second meringue layer; spread with remaining ganache mixture. Top with third meringue layer. Spread reserved whipped-cream mixture on top of meringue layers; decorate with chocolate curls. Fill and serve the same day. Refrigerate until served. Makes 6 to 8 servings.

Top to bottom: Windmill Cake, Chocolate-Filled Meringue Layers

Ganache Crème

2/3 cup whipping cream
11 oz. semisweet or sweet chocolate, coarsely chopped

1. In a medium saucepan over medium heat, heat cream until tiny bubbles form around edge of pan. Remove from heat.
2. Stir in chocolate until mixture is smooth. Makes about 2 cups.

How to use Ganache Crème

1. While still warm, pour over sponge cakes to make a frosting. Let stand until set.
2. Cool 1 to 2 hours or until thickened. Chilled ganache is very stiff; do not use a hand mixer for beating. Beat mixture in a heavy-duty mixer until fluffy. Use as a cake filling and frosting.
3. Cool; refrigerate 4 hours or until firm. Beat mixture in a heavy-duty mixer until fluffy. Fold in whipped cream. Use as a filling or frosting. Or spoon into a pastry bag; use for decorations.

Left to right: Tipsy Cake, Ganache Torte

Ganache Torte

Cake:
4 eggs, separated
1/2 cup plus 1 tablespoon sugar
1/3 cup all-purpose flour
1/3 cup cornstarch

Syrup:
1/4 cup sugar
1/4 cup water
3 tablespoons dark rum

Frosting & Decoration:
2/3 cup whipping cream
1 recipe Ganache Crème, opposite, chilled
12 small chocolate wedges, page 7
Chocolate curls, page 7

---

1. Preheat oven to 350F (175C). Grease 2 (8-inch) round cake pans. Line bottom of pans with waxed or parchment paper; grease paper.
2. Place egg yolks and 1/2 cup sugar in a large bowl set over a pan of simmering water; let stand 5 minutes or until barely warm to the touch. Beat mixture about 10 minutes or until thick and doubled in volume. Remove bowl from pan.
3. Beat until mixture is completely cool. Sift flour and cornstarch into a medium bowl. Set aside. In a medium bowl, beat egg whites with remaining 1 tablespoon sugar until stiff but not dry. Fold beaten egg whites and flour mixture alternately into egg-yolk mixture. Pour batter into prepared pans; smooth tops.
4. Bake in preheated oven 25 to 30 minutes or until a wooden pick inserted in centers comes out clean. Cool in pans on wire racks 5 minutes. Remove from pans; peel off lining paper. Cool completely on wire racks. Cut each layer in half horizontally.
5. To make syrup, in a small saucepan over medium heat, stir sugar and water until sugar dissolves. Boil rapidly 1 minute. Remove from heat; stir in rum. Sprinkle each layer with 2 tablespoons rum syrup.
6. In a medium bowl, beat cream until soft peaks form. Spoon 1/2 of whipped cream into a pastry bag fitted with a medium star or rosette tip; refrigerate. Beat Ganache Crème with a heavy-duty mixer until softened. Beat remaining whipped cream into softened Ganache Crème until thoroughly blended. Reserve 1/2 of ganache mixture to frost cake.
7. Place 1 cake layer on a serving plate; spread with a thin layer of ganache mixture. Top with second cake layer; spread with another thin layer of ganache mixture. Repeat with remaining layers and ganache mixture, ending with cake layer. Press cake down firmly. Spread reserved ganache mixture around side and over top of cake; smooth with a flat spatula.
8. Refrigerate until frosting is set. Score top of cake into 12 equal wedges. Pipe small whipped-cream rosettes in center of each wedge and 1 large rosette in center of cake. Decorate rosettes with chocolate wedges and chocolate curls. Refrigerate until served. Makes 12 servings.

Tipsy Cake

3/4 cup butter or margarine, room temperature
1 cup granulated sugar
3 eggs
1-1/3 cups all-purpose flour
1/3 cup unsweetened cocoa powder
1 teaspoon baking powder
1/4 teaspoon baking soda
1/4 teaspoon salt
1/3 cup milk
1 (16-oz.) can pitted red tart cherries or dark sweet cherries
1/4 cup sweet sherry
1 pint whipping cream (2 cups)
3 tablespoons powdered sugar

To decorate:
Chocolate leaves, page 7
8 to 10 maraschino cherries

---

1. Preheat oven to 350F (175C). Grease and flour a 6-1/2-cup ring mold.
2. In a medium bowl, beat butter or margarine and granulated sugar until light and fluffy. Beat in eggs, 1 at a time, beating well after each addition.
3. Sift flour, cocoa, baking powder, baking soda and salt into a medium bowl. Add flour mixture to sugar mixture alternately with milk, beating until blended. Spread mixture evenly in prepared pan.
4. Bake in preheated oven 40 to 45 minutes or until a wooden pick inserted in center of cake comes out clean. Cool in pan on a wire rack 5 minutes. Remove from pan; cool completely on wire rack.
5. Place cake, top-side down, on a serving plate. Cut a 1-inch slice from top of inverted cake; set slice aside. Scoop out an area 1-inch wide and 1-inch deep in center of remaining cake, reserving crumbs for another use.
6. Drain cherries, reserving 1/4 cup syrup. Stir 2 tablespoons sherry into reserved cherry syrup. Spoon sherry mixture inside cake hollow.
7. In a large bowl, beat cream until soft peaks form. Beat in powdered sugar and remaining 2 tablespoons sherry. Fill cake with 1/4 of whipped-cream mixture.
8. Spoon cherries over whipped-cream mixture. Replace top layer; press down gently. Spread remaining whipped-cream mixture over cake, covering cake completely. Decorate cake with chocolate leaves and maraschino cherries. Refrigerate up to 4 hours. Makes 8 servings.

Chocolate Savarin

1 (1/4-oz.) pkg. active dry yeast (1 tablespoon)
3 tablespoons sugar
1/2 cup warm milk (110F, 45C)
2 cups sifted all-purpose flour
1/2 teaspoon salt
2 eggs, beaten
6 tablespoons butter or margarine, melted, cooled

Syrup:
1/2 cup sugar
3/4 cup water
1 tablespoon instant coffee powder
1 tablespoon unsweetened cocoa powder
2 tablespoons boiling water
2 tablespoons brandy

To decorate:
Julienned orange peel
1 large orange, thinly sliced

---

1. Grease a 9-inch (6-1/2-cup) ring mold or savarin mold.
2. In a large bowl, dissolve yeast and 1 teaspoon sugar in warm milk. Stir to dissolve. Let stand 5 to 10 minutes or until foamy.
3. Stir in remaining sugar, 1 cup flour and salt until blended. Beat in eggs and butter or margarine until blended. Beat in remaining 1 cup flour with a wooden spoon to make a smooth elastic dough.
4. Spoon dough into greased mold; smooth top. Cover with a clean towel. Let rise in a warm place, free from drafts, until dough has risen to within 1 inch of pan rim.
5. Preheat oven to 375F (190C).
6. Bake in preheated oven 30 to 35 minutes or until golden brown. Remove from pan; place on a wire rack.
7. To make syrup, in a medium saucepan over medium heat, stir sugar and 3/4 cup water until sugar dissolves. Bring to a boil; reduce heat. Simmer 5 minutes without stirring.
8. In a small bowl, dissolve coffee and cocoa in boiling water. Stir coffee mixture and brandy into sugar syrup.
9. Place warm savarin in a deep serving plate; prick all over with prongs of a fork. Spoon syrup over savarin; let stand until syrup is completely absorbed.
10. Arrange orange slices in center of savarin; decorate top of savarin with orange peel. Makes 6 to 8 servings.

Mocha Cheesecake

Crust:
1 cup graham-cracker crumbs (14 squares)
2 tablespoons granulated sugar
1/4 cup butter or margarine, melted, cooled

Filling:
2 cups small-curd cottage cheese
5 teaspoons instant coffee powder
2 tablespoons boiling water
1/3 cup butter or margarine, room temperature
3/4 cup granulated sugar
3 eggs, separated
1/4 cup half and half
2 tablespoons cornstarch
4 oz. semisweet chocolate, coarsely chopped

To decorate:
Powdered sugar
Shaved chocolate

---

1. Preheat oven to 325F (165C). Grease bottom and side of a 9-inch springform pan.
2. To make crust, in a small bowl, combine cracker crumbs, sugar and butter or margarine. Press crumbs onto bottom of greased pan. Refrigerate while preparing filling.
3. To make filling, discard any liquid from cottage cheese. In a blender or food processor fitted with a steel blade, process cottage cheese until smooth. In a small bowl, dissolve coffee in boiling water; let cool.
4. In a large bowl, beat butter or margarine and sugar until light and fluffy. Beat in egg yolks until blended. Beat in cooled coffee and half and half until blended. Beat in cornstarch and pureed cottage cheese until combined. Fold in chocolate.
5. In a medium bowl, beat egg whites until stiff but not dry. Fold beaten egg whites into cheese mixture. Pour mixture over chilled crust; smooth top.
6. Bake in preheated oven 1 hour 10 minutes to 1 hour 20 minutes or until center is set. Turn oven off; let cheesecake cool in oven 2 hours with oven door slightly propped open. Cheesecake will fall slightly. Refrigerate until completely chilled.
7. Run tip of a knife around inside edge of pan; remove side of pan. Place cheesecake on a serving plate. Sift powdered sugar over top immediately before serving. Decorate center with chocolate shavings. Makes 8 to 10 servings.

Left to right: Mocha Cheesecake, Chocolate Savarin

Chocolate Slice

3 eggs
3 tablespoons warm water
1/2 cup sugar
1 teaspoon vanilla extract
3/4 cup cake flour
Double recipe Special Buttercream, opposite
6 tablespoons unsweetened cocoa powder, sifted
2/3 cup finely chopped, toasted, blanched almonds

1. Preheat oven to 375F (190C). Grease a 13" x 9" baking pan. Line bottom of pan with waxed paper. Grease and flour paper.
2. In a medium bowl, beat eggs and warm water until foamy. Beat in sugar; beat 10 minutes or until thick and lemon-colored. Mixture should fall in a thick ribbon when beaters are lifted. Beat in vanilla.
3. Sift flour over egg mixture; fold in. Pour mixture into prepared pan; spread evenly.
4. Bake in preheated oven 15 to 18 minutes or until center of cake springs back when lightly pressed. Cool in pan on a wire rack 5 minutes. Remove from pan; peel off lining paper. Cool completely on wire rack. Cut cake crosswise into 3 equal strips, each about 4 inches wide.
5. Prepare Special Buttercream as directed opposite. Add cocoa; beat until blended. Refrigerate until firm enough to spread.
6. Spoon 1/3 of buttercream into a pastry bag fitted with a coupling. Attach a small plain writing tip; refrigerate. Place 1 cake strip on a serving plate; spread with a thin layer of buttercream. Top with second cake strip; spread with buttercream. Place third cake strip on top. Spread remaining buttercream around sides and over top of cake. Press almonds lightly into buttercream on sides of cake.
7. Pipe chilled buttercream in thin diagonal lines across top of cake. Change to an open star tip; pipe a shell border around top edge of cake. Makes 6 to 8 servings.

Top to bottom: Chocolate Slice, Praline Roll

Praline Roll

Cake:
3 eggs
3 tablespoons warm water
1/2 cup granulated sugar
1 teaspoon vanilla extract
3/4 cup cake flour
Powdered sugar

Filling:
1 recipe Special Buttercream, opposite
1/2 recipe Praline, page 49, crushed

Icing:
1-1/2 cups sifted powdered sugar
3 tablespoons unsweetened cocoa powder
1 to 2 tablespoons water or light rum

1. Preheat oven to 375F (190C). Grease a 13" x 9" baking pan. Line bottom of pan with waxed paper. Grease and flour paper.
2. To make cake, in a medium bowl, beat eggs and warm water until foamy. Beat in granulated sugar; beat 10 minutes or until thick and lemon-colored. Mixture should fall in a thick ribbon when beaters are lifted. Beat in vanilla.
3. Sift flour over egg mixture; fold in. Pour mixture into prepared pan; spread evenly.
4. Bake in preheated oven 15 to 18 minutes or until center springs back when lightly pressed.
5. Sift powdered sugar over a clean towel; invert cake onto sugared towel. Peel off lining paper; trim crusty edges. Starting from short end, roll up cake in towel. Cool completely on a wire rack.
6. To make filling, prepare buttercream as directed opposite. Refrigerate until firm. Spoon 1/3 cup buttercream into a pastry bag fitted with an open-star tip; refrigerate. Fold crushed praline into remaining buttercream.
7. Unroll cake; spread praline-buttercream mixture over cake to within 1/2 inch of edges. Reroll cake, without towel; place, seam-side down, on a flat plate. Cover and refrigerate 1 hour.
8. To make icing, in a medium bowl, combine powdered sugar, cocoa and water or rum. Stir until smooth and icing is a good consistency for pouring. Place cake on a wire rack set over a baking sheet. Spoon icing over cake; spread evenly with a flat spatula.
9. Place cake on a serving plate; let stand until icing is set. Pipe chilled buttercream into scrolls on top of cake. Makes 6 to 8 servings.

Special Buttercream

5 tablespoons sugar
1/2 cup water
1 egg yolk
10 tablespoons unsalted butter, cubed
1/2 teaspoon vanilla extract

1. In a small saucepan over medium heat, stir sugar and water until sugar dissolves.
2. Boil rapidly about 3 minutes, without stirring. Continue boiling until syrup forms a thread when dropped from a spoon onto a plate or to 225F (105C) on a candy thermometer.
3. Place egg yolk in a medium bowl; gradually beat in hot syrup, beating until mixture cools.
4. Gradually beat in butter, a little at a time, until smooth. Beat in vanilla. Refrigerate to firm, if necessary. Makes about 1-1/2 cups.

Variation
Beat in 2 tablespoons coffee-flavored liqueur or orange-flavored liqueur with vanilla.

Sponge Layers

4 eggs
1/2 cup sugar
1 teaspoon vanilla extract
3/4 cup cake flour

1. Preheat oven to 350F (175C). Grease 2 (8-inch) round cake pans. Line bottoms with parchment paper or waxed paper; grease paper. Dust pans with flour; tap out excess.
2. In a medium bowl, beat eggs and sugar 10 minutes or until thick and lemon-colored. Mixture should fall in a thick ribbon when beaters are lifted. Beat in vanilla.
3. Sift flour over egg mixture; fold in. Pour mixture into prepared pans; spread evenly.
4. Bake in preheated oven 20 to 25 minutes or until centers spring back when lightly pressed. Cool in pans on wire racks 5 minutes. Remove from pans; peel off lining paper. Cool completely on wire racks. Fill and frost as desired. Makes 2 layers.

Orange & Chocolate Cake

Cake:
1 recipe Genoise Layers, opposite
Grated peel of 1 orange

Filling:
2/3 cup whipping cream
5 oz. semisweet or sweet chocolate, coarsely chopped
1 to 2 tablespoons Cointreau

Frosting:
1/4 cup butter or margarine
1/3 cup firmly packed light-brown sugar
Grated peel of 1 orange
2 tablespoons orange juice
2-1/4 cups sifted powdered sugar

To decorate:
Shaved chocolate, page 7
Powdered sugar

---

1. Preheat oven 350F (175C). Grease and line 2 (8-inch) round cake pans. Prepare and bake Genoise Layers as directed opposite, adding orange peel with flour. Cool in pans on wire racks 5 minutes. Remove from pans; peel off lining paper. Cool completely on wire racks.
2. To make filling, in a small saucepan over low heat, heat cream until tiny bubbles form around edge of pan. Remove from heat; stir in chocolate until mixture is smooth. Stir in Cointreau to taste. Cool slightly; refrigerate until set.
3. To make frosting, in a small saucepan over low heat, combine butter or margarine, brown sugar, orange peel and orange juice. Cook, stirring, until butter or margarine melts and sugar dissolves. Boil 1 minute, stirring.
4. Place powdered sugar in a medium bowl. Beat in hot brown-sugar mixture with a wooden spoon until blended and smooth.
5. Place 1 cake layer, bottom-side up, on a plate; spread with chilled chocolate filling. Top with second layer, bottom-side down; press down lightly. Place cake on a wire rack set over a baking sheet. Spoon frosting over cake, letting frosting run down side of cake. Smooth with a flat spatula; let stand until frosting is set. Sift powdered sugar over top of cake; decorate with chocolate shavings. Makes 6 to 8 servings.

Chocolate-Strawberry Valentine

1 recipe Genoise Layers, opposite
1/4 cup finely ground hazelnuts or almonds

Filling & Decoration:
1 pint strawberries, washed, hulled
1/2 pint whipping cream (1 cup)
2 tablespoons powdered sugar
2 oz. semisweet or sweet chocolate, grated
1 recipe warm Ganache Crème, page 38

To decorate:
Chocolate leaves, page 7

---

1. Grease 2 (8-inch) heart-shaped pans. Line bottoms of pans with parchment paper or waxed paper; grease paper. Dust pans with flour; tap out excess flour.
2. Prepare and bake Genoise Layers in prepared heart-shaped pans as directed opposite, adding hazelnuts or almonds with flour. Cool in pans on wire racks 5 minutes. Remove from pans; peel off lining paper. Cool completely on wire racks. Cut each cake layer in half horizontally to make a total of 4 layers.
3. Set aside 3 whole strawberries for decoration. Slice enough strawberries to make 24 thin slices for decoration; set aside. Chop remaining strawberries.
4. In a medium bowl, beat cream until soft peaks form. Beat in powdered sugar. Fold in chocolate and reserved chopped strawberries.
5. Place 1 cake layer on a flat work surface; spread with 1/3 of strawberry-cream mixture. Top with second layer; spread with 1/3 of strawberry-cream mixture. Repeat with remaining layers and strawberry-cream mixture, ending with a cake layer.
6. Place filled cake on a wire rack set over a baking sheet. Pour warm Ganache Crème over cake, covering completely. Smooth with a flat spatula. Let stand 30 minutes.
7. Arrange sliced strawberries around bottom edge of cake. Decorate top of cake with reserved whole strawberries and chocolate leaves. Let cake stand on wire rack; refrigerate until Genache Crème is completely set. Slide a wide flat spatula under cake. Lift cake from rack; place on a serving plate. Fill and serve cake the same day. Makes 6 to 8 servings.

Left to right: Orange & Chocolate Cake, Chocolate-Strawberry
Valentine

Genoise Layers

4 eggs
2/3 cup superfine sugar
3/4 cup cake flour, sifted
1/4 cup sweet butter, melted, cooled

1. Preheat oven to 350F (175C). Grease 2 (8-inch) round cake pans. Line bottoms with parchment paper or waxed paper; grease paper. Dust pans with flour; tap out excess flour.

2. Place eggs in a large bowl set over a pan of simmering water; let stand about 5 minutes or until barely warm to the touch. Beat eggs until foamy. Gradually beat in sugar. Beat about 10 minutes or until mixture is thick and doubled in volume. Remove bowl from pan.

3. Beat mixture until cold. Gradually sift flour over mixture; fold in. Fold in butter only until streaks disappear. Pour mixture into prepared pans; smooth tops.

4. Bake in preheated oven 20 to 25 minutes or until centers spring back when lightly pressed. Cool in pans on wire racks 5 minutes. Remove from pans; peel off lining paper. Cool completely on wire racks. Use immediately, or wrap in foil or freezer paper and freeze for use at another time. Makes 6 to 8 servings.

Meringue Basket

6 egg whites
1/4 teaspoon cream of tartar
1/2 cup superfine sugar
1 cup powdered sugar
3 tablespoons unsweetened cocoa powder
1 teaspoon vanilla extract

Filling:
8 oz. semisweet chocolate, chopped
1 tablespoon milk
4 egg yolks
2 tablespoons coffee-flavored liqueur
1-3/4 cups whipping cream
3 tablespoons powdered sugar
Chocolate sprinkles
1 pint fresh raspberries (2 cups)

1. Preheat oven to 225F (105C). Line 2 baking sheets with parchment paper. Draw 4 (8-inch) squares on parchment paper.
2. In a large bowl, beat egg whites and cream of tartar with an electric mixer at high speed until soft peaks form. Gradually beat in superfine sugar; beat until meringue is stiff and glossy. Sift powdered sugar and cocoa over meringue; fold in. Fold in vanilla.
3. Spoon meringue into a pastry bag fitted with a plain 1/2-inch writing tip. Pipe out meringue inside outlines of all 4 squares on parchment paper, making a strip 1/2-inch wide. Pipe meringue inside 2 squares until completely filled; spread evenly, covering bottom of squares completely.
4. Bake in preheated oven 2 hours or until meringues are completely dry. Cool on baking sheets 5 minutes. Carefully peel off lining paper; cool completely on wire racks.
5. To make filling, melt 7 ounces chocolate in a small heavy saucepan over very low heat; stir until smooth. Stir in milk until blended. Beat in egg yolks, 1 at a time, beating well after each addition. Stir in liqueur. Refrigerate about 1 hour or until completely cool and set.
6. In a medium bowl, beat cream until soft peaks form. Beat in powdered sugar. Place 1 solid meringue square on a flat serving plate; spread with a thin layer of whipped-cream mixture. Top with 1 open meringue square. Spread a little whipped-cream mixture on edges of square; top with remaining open meringue square. See illustration opposite.
7. Spread whipped-cream mixture around sides of square. Draw an icing comb over each side to create a serrated effect. Use a small spatula to press a narrow band of chocolate sprinkles around bottom of meringue basket.
8. Spoon chilled chocolate mixture into center of meringue basket. Set 12 raspberries aside for decoration. Arrange remaining raspberries on top of chocolate filling.
9. Spread a thin layer of whipped-cream mixture over remaining solid meringue square; place at an angle on top of raspberries, cream-covered-side up.

10. Spoon remaining whipped-cream mixture into a pastry bag fitted with a 1/8-inch plain writing tip. Pipe whipped-cream mixture in diagonal lines on top of meringue basket.
11. Melt remaining 1 ounce chocolate in a small heavy saucepan over very low heat; stir until melted. Cool slightly; drizzle chocolate on top of meringue basket. Arrange reserved raspberries over top, if desired. Assemble and serve the same day. Refrigerate until served. Makes 8 to 10 servings.

Variations

Pipe about 3/4 cup meringue into 4 (8-inch) ribbons on lined baking sheet, using a serrated ribbon tip, if desired. Bake with meringue squares. In step 11, decorate edge of basket with meringue ribbons after drizzling chocolate over top of basket.

Meringue Nests: Use 3 egg whites and 3/4 cup sugar. Prepare meringue as directed in step 2. Spoon meringue into a pastry bag fitted with a 1/2-inch star tip. Pipe about 10 small meringue nests, about 4 inches in diameter, on parchment-lined baking sheets. Bake as directed in step 4 opposite. To fill, beat 1/2 pint (1 cup) whipping cream until soft peaks form; beat in 2 tablespoons powdered sugar. Decorate with sliced strawberries and grated chocolate.

1/Top with remaining open meringue square.

2/Draw an icing comb over each side to create a serrated effect.

3/Spoon chilled chocolate mixture into center of meringue basket.

Paris Brest au Chocolat

1 recipe Choux Pastry, page 35
1/4 cup sliced almonds
Powdered sugar

Chocolate-Cream Filling:
2 tablespoons cornstarch
1/3 cup granulated sugar
1 cup milk
3 egg yolks, beaten
3 oz. semisweet chocolate, melted
1 teaspoon vanilla extract
1/2 pint whipping cream (1 cup)
2 tablespoons powdered sugar
1/2 recipe Praline, opposite, crushed

---

1. Preheat oven to 400F (205C). Line a baking sheet with parchment paper. Draw an 8- or 9-inch circle on parchment paper.
2. Prepare choux paste as directed on page 35. Spoon choux paste into a pastry bag fitted with a 3/4-inch plain writing tip. Pipe out choux paste into a 1-1/4-inch-wide ring inside circle on lined baking sheet. Sprinkle with almonds.
3. Bake in preheated oven 35 to 40 minutes or until puffed and golden brown. Remove from baking sheet; cool on a wire rack.
4. To make filling, in a medium saucepan, combine cornstarch and granulated sugar. Gradually stir in milk until blended and smooth. Cook over low heat, stirring, until mixture thickens and comes to a boil. Remove from heat; stir 1/4 cup hot milk mixture into egg yolks until blended. Return mixture to saucepan; cook, stirring, until mixture is thickened. Do not boil. Pour custard into a large bowl. Stir in chocolate and vanilla until blended. Cover surface of custard with a sheet of waxed paper to prevent a skin from forming. Refrigerate 2 to 3 hours or until completely chilled.
5. In a medium bowl, beat cream until soft peaks form. Beat in powdered sugar. Fold whipped-cream mixture into chilled chocolate custard; fold in praline.
6. Split choux ring horizontally, making bottom part slightly thicker. Remove and discard any soft dough from inside. Fill bottom of ring with chocolate-cream filling. Replace top; sift powdered sugar over filled ring. Fill and serve the same day. Refrigerate until served. Makes 6 to 8 servings.

Mocha & Praline Gâteau

Cake:
4 oz. semisweet chocolate
1 teaspoon instant coffee powder
1/4 cup water
5 eggs
2/3 cup sugar
1 cup cake flour, sifted

Buttercream:
1/2 cup butter or margarine, room temperature
4 oz. unsweetened chocolate, melted, cooled
2 egg yolks
4 cups powdered sugar, sifted
2 to 3 tablespoons coffee-flavored liqueur

To decorate:
1 recipe Praline, opposite, crushed
Chocolate curls

---

1. Preheat oven to 350F (175C). Grease 2 (8-inch) round cake pans. Line bottoms of pans with waxed paper. Grease and flour paper and sides of pans.
2. To prepare cake, in a small heavy saucepan over low heat, stir chocolate, coffee and water until chocolate melts and mixture is smooth. Set aside to cool.
3. Place eggs in a large bowl set over a pan of barely simmering water. Let stand about 5 minutes or until barely warm to the touch. Beat eggs until foamy. Gradually beat in sugar. Beat about 10 minutes or until mixture is thick and doubled in volume. Remove bowl from pan.
4. Add flour to egg mixture alternately with cooled chocolate mixture; beat until blended. Pour batter into prepared pans; smooth tops.
5. Bake in preheated oven 25 to 30 minutes or until center springs back when lightly pressed. Cool in pans on a wire rack 10 minutes. Remove from pans; peel off lining paper. Cool completely on wire rack.
6. To make buttercream, in a medium bowl, beat butter or margarine, chocolate and egg yolks until blended. Gradually beat in powdered sugar and liqueur; beat until frosting is fluffy and a good consistency for spreading. Spoon 2/3 cup frosting into a pastry bag fitted with a small star tip. Refrigerate frosting until ready to use.
7. Cut cooled cake layers in half horizontally. Place 1 layer, bottom-side up, on a serving plate; spread with a thin layer of buttercream. Top with second half of layer; spread with buttercream. Repeat with remaining layers and buttercream. Spread a thin layer of buttercream around side and over top of cake. Press crushed praline lightly around side of cake. Pipe reserved buttercream decoratively around top edge of cake; decorate with chocolate curls. Makes 6 to 8 servings.

Praline

**1/2 cup sugar
1 cup almonds or hazelnuts**

Praline is usually made with almonds or hazelnuts. When making praline, carefully watch to prevent the nuts from burning when they are placed in the caramelized sugar. Use a well-greased wooden spoon or spatula to turn the nuts. Do not touch hot praline with your fingers!

1. Butter a jelly-roll pan or baking sheet; set aside. Lightly grease a wooden spoon or spatula; set aside.

2. Place sugar in a heavy medium saucepan or skillet over low heat. Cook, stirring, until sugar dissolves and is golden caramel in color.

3. Stir in nuts with greased wooden spoon or spatula until completely coated and sugar is deep caramel in color.

4. Pour mixture onto prepared pan. Let stand until completely hard. Break praline into pieces. For finely crushed praline, in a blender or food processor fitted with a steel blade, process praline pieces until crushed. Or, place praline between 2 sheets of waxed paper; crush by striking with a rolling pin. Makes about 1/2 pound praline or 1-1/3 cups crushed praline.

Variation
Substitute walnuts, pecans or pistachios for almonds or hazelnuts.

Left to right: Crowning Glory, page 32; Paris Brest au Chocolat

Top to bottom: Chocolate Basket, Chocolate-Bran Cake

Chocolate Basket

1 recipe Cocoa Layer Cake, opposite
2 recipes Chocolate Buttercream, opposite
About 24 chocolate leaves, page 7
About 12 red candied cherries, some halved, some
  quartered
Powdered sugar, if desired

1. Prepare, bake and cool cake as directed opposite. Cut each cooled cake layer in half horizontally to make 4 layers. Place 1 cake layer on a serving plate; spread with a thin layer of buttercream. Top with another cake layer; spread with a thin layer of buttercream. Repeat with a third layer and more buttercream.

2. Using a 6-inch circle as a guide, cut a circle from center of remaining layer. Remove circle; set aside. Place cake ring on the top of the cake. Fill center of ring with buttercream.
3. Spoon remaining buttercream into a pastry bag fitted with a ribbon tip. Pipe a basketwork design on the side of the cake and on top and side of 6-inch cake circle.
4. Carefully arrange chocolate leaves, almost touching, on top of cake ring. Place cherries between leaves.
5. Carefully place small decorated cake circle on buttercream-filled center of cake. Makes 8 to 10 servings.

Chocolate-Bran Cake

Cake:
1/4 cup unprocessed bran flakes
3/4 cup raisins
3/4 cup orange juice
6 tablespoons butter or margarine, room temperature
2/3 cup firmly packed light-brown sugar
2 eggs
1-1/2 cups all-purpose flour
1/4 cup unsweetened cocoa powder
2 teaspoons baking powder
1/2 teaspoon baking soda
1/2 teaspoon freshly grated nutmeg
1/2 teaspoon salt
1/2 cup chopped walnuts

Filling & Topping:
1/2 (8-oz.) pkg. cream cheese, room temperature
2 tablespoons milk
3 oz. semisweet chocolate, melted, cooled
About 1/3 cup powdered sugar
Walnut halves

1. Preheat oven to 325F (165C). Grease a 9" x 5" loaf pan.
2. In a small bowl, combine bran, raisins and orange juice. Set aside.
3. In a medium bowl, beat butter or margarine and brown sugar 5 to 8 minutes or until light and fluffy. Beat in eggs until blended.
4. Sift flour, cocoa, baking powder, baking soda, nutmeg and salt over egg mixture; stir in with a wooden spoon until blended.
5. Stir in reserved bran mixture until combined. Fold in walnuts. Pour mixture into greased pan; smooth top.
6. Bake in preheated oven 60 to 65 minutes or until a wooden pick inserted in center comes out clean. Cool in pan on a wire rack 10 minutes. Remove from pan; cool completely on wire rack.
7. To make filling, in a medium bowl, beat cream cheese and milk until fluffy. Beat in chocolate until blended. Beat in 1/4 cup powdered sugar.
8. Cut cake in half horizontally to make 2 layers. Place bottom layer on a serving plate; spread with chocolate filling, reserving 1 to 2 tablespoons. Top with remaining layer. Spread flat sides of walnuts with reserved filling; place down center of cake. Sift 1 to 2 tablespoons powdered sugar over cake. Makes 8 to 10 servings.

Cocoa Layer Cake

3/4 cup butter or margarine, room temperature
1-1/4 cups sugar
4 eggs
1 teaspoon vanilla extract
1-1/2 cups cake flour
1/2 cup unsweetened cocoa powder
1-1/4 teaspoons baking soda
1/2 teaspoon salt
1/2 cup milk

1. Preheat oven to 350F (175C). Grease and flour 2 (8-inch) round cake pans.
2. In a large bowl, beat butter or margarine and sugar 5 to 8 minutes or until light and fluffy. Beat in eggs and vanilla until blended.
3. Sift flour, cocoa, baking soda and salt into a medium bowl. Add flour mixture to egg mixture alternately with milk; beat until blended. Pour batter into prepared pans; smooth tops.
4. Bake in preheated oven 25 to 35 minutes or until centers spring back when lightly pressed. Cool in pans on wire racks 5 minutes. Remove from pans; cool completely on wire racks. Fill and frost as desired. Makes 2 layers.

Chocolate Buttercream

2 tablespoons unsweetened cocoa powder
2 tablespoons boiling water
1/2 cup butter or margarine, room temperature
2 cups powdered sugar, sifted
1 tablespoon half and half

1. In a small bowl, blend cocoa and boiling water into a smooth paste.
2. In a medium bowl, beat butter or margarine until creamy. Beat in 1/2 of powdered sugar until light and fluffy. Beat in cocoa paste, remaining powdered sugar and half and half until fluffy and icing is a good consistency for spreading. Makes about 1-1/2 cups.

Coconut-Nougat Squares

Edible rice paper
1 cup granulated sugar
1 cup firmly packed dark-brown sugar
2/3 cup water
2 egg whites
1 cup toasted flaked or shredded coconut
1/2 cup red candied cherries, chopped
4 oz. semisweet chocolate, chopped

1. Wipe bottom of an 8-inch-square pan with a damp cloth. Cut 2 sheets of rice paper to fit bottom of pan. Line pan bottom with 1 sheet of rice paper, pressing paper onto damp surface of pan.
2. In a medium saucepan over low heat, stir sugars and water until sugar dissolves and mixture comes to a boil. Boil rapidly until mixture reaches the soft-crack stage 270F to 290F (132C to 143C) on a candy thermometer. Remove from heat.
3. In a medium bowl, beat egg whites until stiff but not dry. Gradually pour in hot sugar syrup in a slow steady stream, beating constantly. Beat until stiff and glossy. Fold in coconut and cherries.
4. Pour mixture into lined pan; spread evenly. Cover with remaining sheet of rice paper. Cover rice paper with waxed paper or foil. Place another 8-inch-square pan on top of paper or foil, bottom-side down. Place a 2-pound can or other heavy weight in pan.
5. Refrigerate at least 24 hours. Remove weighted pan and waxed paper or foil; run a knife tip around edge of pan; carefully ease nougat out of pan. Place on a flat work surface; cut into 25 squares.
6. Melt chocolate in a small heavy saucepan over very low heat; stir until smooth. Let cool slightly. Dip squares halfway into melted chocolate. Place on waxed paper or foil; let stand until chocolate is set. Makes 25 squares.

Chocolate & Nut Squares

1 cup all-purpose flour
2 tablespoons unsweetened cocoa powder
1 (3-3/8-oz.) pkg. instant vanilla pudding
1/4 cup sugar
3/4 cup butter or margarine

Topping:
2 tablespoons apricot jam, melted, cooled
6 tablespoons butter or margarine
1/2 cup firmly packed light-brown sugar
1 tablespoon honey
1 oz. semisweet chocolate, chopped
1 cup finely chopped toasted almonds

1. Preheat oven to 300F (150C). Line an 8-inch-square pan with waxed paper or foil; grease paper or foil.
2. Sift flour, cocoa and pudding mix into a medium bowl. Stir in sugar. With a pastry blender or 2 knives, cut in butter or margarine until mixture resembles coarse crumbs. Knead dough in bowl until smooth. Press mixture into bottom of lined pan; prick lightly with a fork.
3. Bake in preheated oven 1 hour 15 minutes or until center is firm when lightly pressed. Cool completely in pan on a wire rack.
4. To make topping, brush jam over cooled cake. In a medium saucepan over medium heat, stir butter or margarine, brown sugar and honey until mixture comes to a boil. Boil 3 minutes, stirring constantly.
5. Remove from heat; stir in chocolate until melted. Stir in nuts. Spread nut mixture over cake; let stand 15 minutes. Score into 25 squares. Cool until topping is firm.
6. Remove from pan; peel off paper or foil. Cut into squares. Makes 25 squares.

Variation
Spread 4 ounces melted semisweet chocolate over nut topping; let stand until set.

Top to bottom: Chocolate & Nut Squares, Coconut-Nougat Squares

Clockwise from left: Chocolate Stars, Caramel Crunch Cookies, Chocolate Fudge

Chocolate Fudge

1/4 cup butter or margarine
4 oz. unsweetened chocolate, chopped
1/3 cup evaporated milk or whipping cream
1 teaspoon vanilla extract
1 (16-oz.) box powdered sugar
1/2 cup chopped nuts, if desired

To decorate:
4 oz. semisweet chocolate, chopped

1. Butter an 8-inch-square pan.
2. Combine butter or margarine, chocolate and evaporated milk or whipping cream in top of a double boiler set over a pan of simmering water. Cook, stirring, until chocolate melts and mixture is smooth. Stir in vanilla. Remove top of double boiler from heat.
3. Sift powdered sugar into a medium bowl; make a well in center. Slowly beat warm chocolate mixture into sugar, beating until mixture is blended and all of powdered sugar has been incorporated. Fold in chopped nuts, if desired.
4. Pour into prepared pan; spread evenly. Refrigerate about 2 hours or until set.
5. To decorate, melt chocolate in a small heavy saucepan over very low heat; stir until smooth. Let cool.
6. Spread melted chocolate over top of chilled fudge; let stand until chocolate is set. Cut into small pieces; remove from pan. Makes 48 to 64 pieces.

Chocolate Stars

Cookies:
1/2 cup butter or margarine, room temperature
3/4 cup sugar
1 egg
1 tablespoon milk
2 teaspoons grated orange peel
1-1/2 cups sifted all-purpose flour
1/4 cup cornstarch
1/4 cup unsweetened cocoa powder
1/2 teaspoon salt

Icing:
1 (16-oz.) box powdered sugar, sifted
1/4 cup orange juice
Few drops orange food coloring
2 tablespoons unsweetened cocoa powder
2 tablespoons boiling water

1. Preheat oven to 350F (175C). Grease 2 baking sheets.
2. In a medium bowl, beat butter or margarine and sugar until light and fluffy. Beat in egg, milk and orange peel until blended.
3. Sift flour, cornstarch, cocoa and salt over sugar mixture. Gradually stir in flour mixture with a wooden spoon to make a soft dough. Knead dough in bowl 8 to 10 strokes or until smooth.
4. Divide dough in half. On a lightly floured surface, roll out 1 piece of dough to 1/4 inch thick. Cut dough with a floured 3-inch star cookie cutter. Place cookies about 1 inch apart on greased baking sheets. Repeat with remaining dough.
5. Bake in preheated oven 12 to 14 minutes or until firm. Remove from baking sheets; cool completely on wire racks.
6. To make icing, in a medium bowl, blend powdered sugar and orange juice until smooth. Spoon 1/2 cup icing into a small bowl; tint with a few drops of orange food coloring.
7. In a small bowl, blend cocoa and boiling water into a smooth paste. Stir cocoa paste into plain icing. If necessary, add a little more powdered sugar to make icing a good consistency for spreading.
8. Spread chocolate icing over tops of cookies. Spoon orange icing into a pastry bag fitted with a small plain writing tip. Pipe orange icing into 4 or 5 circles on top of each cookie. Or, pipe icing in a spiral, starting from center of each cookie.
9. With a fine metal skewer, draw orange icing from center out toward points of stars. Then draw icing back in toward center from between points to give a flower effect. Let stand until icing is set. Makes 36 to 40 cookies.

Caramel Crunch Cookies

Crumb Layer:
1/2 cup butter or margarine
1/2 cup sugar
1/4 cup unsweetened cocoa powder
1 teaspoon vanilla extract
2 cups graham-cracker crumbs
1/3 cup chopped nuts

Caramel Layer:
1 (14-oz.) can sweetened condensed milk
2 tablespoons butter or margarine
3 tablespoons dark corn syrup
1 teaspoon vanilla extract

Topping:
4 oz. semisweet chocolate, chopped

1. Grease an 11" x 7" baking pan.
2. To make crumb layer, in a medium saucepan over low heat, combine butter or margarine, sugar, cocoa and vanilla. Stir until butter or margarine melts and mixture is smooth. Remove from heat. Stir in crumbs and nuts until combined.
3. Press crumb mixture onto bottom of greased pan; smooth top.
4. To make caramel layer, in a small saucepan over low heat, combine condensed milk, butter or margarine, corn syrup and vanilla. Stir until mixture comes to a boil. Boil 3 minutes, stirring constantly. Pour hot caramel over crumb layer. Spread evenly; let stand until completely cool.
5. Melt chocolate in a small heavy saucepan over very low heat; stir until smooth. Let cool. Spread cooled chocolate over caramel layer. Let stand until chocolate is set. Run a knife tip around inside of pan to loosen mixture. Cut into 25 bars. Makes 25 cookies.

Finger Cookies with Chocolate Dip

Cookies:
1-1/3 cups all-purpose flour
1/2 cup sugar
1/4 cup finely ground blanched almonds
2 teaspoons grated lemon peel
2/3 cup butter or margarine
1 egg
1 tablespoon milk

Chocolate Dip:
7 oz. semisweet, sweet or milk chocolate, coarsely
   chopped
2 tablespoons butter or margarine
1/2 cup milk
1/4 cup ground toasted almonds, if desired

---

1. Preheat oven to 350F (175C). Grease a baking sheet.
2. To make cookies, in a medium bowl, combine flour, sugar, almonds, and lemon peel. With a pastry cutter or 2 knives, cut in butter or margarine until mixture resembles coarse crumbs. In a small bowl, beat egg and milk until blended; sprinkle over flour mixture. Stir with a fork until mixture binds together. Knead dough in bowl 8 to 10 strokes or until smooth.
3. On a lightly floured surface, roll out pastry to a 10" x 8" rectangle about 1/4 inch thick. Cut pastry crosswise into 2 (8" x 5") rectangles. Cut each rectangle in half lengthwise to make 4 (5" x 4") rectangles. Cut each rectangle into 10 (4" x 1/2") fingers. Place fingers about 1/2 inch apart on greased baking sheet.
4. Bake in preheated oven 12 to 15 minutes or until golden. Remove from baking sheet; cool completely on a wire rack.
5. To make chocolate dip, melt chocolate and butter or margarine in a medium heavy saucepan over low heat. Stir until mixture is smooth. Gradually stir in milk; beat until mixture is smooth. Remove from heat; stir in almonds, if desired.
6. Pour chocolate dip into a serving bowl; cool to room temperature. If desired, divide cookies into 6 to 8 portions. Wrap portions in fancy paper napkins. Or, serve individually. Makes 6 to 8 servings.

Mushroom Cake

1/2 recipe Cocoa Layer Cake, page 51
1 recipe Chocolate Buttercream, page 51
8 oz. marzipan
2 tablespoons apricot jam, melted
Powdered sugar

---

1. Prepare and bake cake in an 8-inch-round cake pan as directed on page 51. Cool on a wire rack.
2. Prepare buttercream as directed on page 51. Spoon into a pastry bag fitted with a large star tip. Pipe lines of buttercream from edge of cake to the center until entire top is covered.
3. Reserve 1 ounce of marzipan. To measure marzipan for cake, cut 2 pieces of string, one 1/2-inch longer than cake is tall and the other the exact distance around cake. Roll remaining marzipan into a rope about 24 inches long. Roll out marzipan into a strip that will reach around cake and extend about 1/2 inch above top. Trim rolled marzipan to size, using pieces of string for measuring.
4. Brush side of cake with jam. Roll up marzipan. Place one end of marzipan on side of cake. Carefully unroll around cake, pressing against side of cake. Use a small spatula to blend seam line. Gently push marzipan that extends above cake inward so it curves slightly over piped buttercream.
5. Shape reserved marzipan into a stem; place in center of cake. Sift powdered sugar over cake. Makes 6 servings.

Variation
Chocolate Butterflies: Spoon cake batter into a muffin pan lined with paper baking cups. Bake in preheated 375F (190C) oven about 15 to 20 minutes or until cupcakes spring back when pressed. Cool on a wire rack. When cool, remove paper cups. Cut a 1/2-inch slice from top of each cupcake, using a sharp knife. Cut each small slice in half. Spoon or pipe a little buttercream into center of each cupcake, using a star tip. Press 2 halves, rounded-side down, into buttercream to resemble butterfly wings. Sift powdered sugar over tops. Decorate with candied fruit, chopped nuts or chocolate curls. Makes 12 to 14 cupcakes.

Surprise Cones

10 small ice-cream cones
1/2 cup chopped mixed nuts
2 cups miniature marshmallows
7 oz. milk chocolate, broken into pieces
1/4 cup milk or evaporated milk

To decorate:
1/4 to 1/2 cup sprinkles

1. If cones have pointed bottoms, place in something to hold them upright. Place flat-bottomed cones on a baking sheet.
2. Sprinkle 1/2 of nuts in bottoms of cones.
3. In a small bowl, combine remaining 1/4 cup nuts and marshmallows.
4. In a small saucepan over low heat, stir chocolate and milk until mixture is smooth. Set aside about 30 minutes or until cool, but still soft.
5. Stir chocolate mixture into marshmallows and nuts; let stand about 1 hour or until completely cold, but still sticky.
6. Immediately before serving, place about 2 tablespoons of chocolate mixture in each cone; round top.
7. Dip top of each cone into sprinkles; serve immediately. Makes 10 small cones.

Right to left: Surprise Cones, Finger Cookies with Chocolate Dip, Mushroom Cake

Left to right: Peppermint Marble Cake, Chocolate-Fudge Bars, Chocolate-Covered Peanutty Bars

Peppermint Marble Cake

3/4 cup butter or margarine, room temperature
1 cup granulated sugar
3 eggs
1-2/3 cups all-purpose flour
1 teaspoon baking powder
1/2 teaspoon baking soda
2 tablespoons unsweetened cocoa powder
2 teaspoons instant coffee powder
2 tablespoons boiling water
1/2 teaspoon vanilla extract
1/2 teaspoon peppermint extract
2 to 3 drops green food coloring
Powdered sugar

1. Preheat oven to 350F (175C). Grease a 6-1/2-cup ring mold.
2. In a medium bowl, beat butter or margarine and granulated sugar until light and fluffy. Beat in eggs, 1 at a time, beating well after each addition.
3. Sift flour, baking powder and baking soda over egg mixture; fold in. Divide batter into thirds, placing batter in 2 additional bowls.
4. In a small bowl, dissolve cocoa and coffee in boiling water; stir into 1 bowl of batter. Stir vanilla into second bowl of batter. Stir peppermint extract and green food coloring into third bowl of batter.
5. Spoon batters alternately into greased pan. Run tip of a knife through batters to create a marbled effect.
6. Bake in preheated oven 40 to 45 minutes or until a wooden pick inserted in center comes out clean. Cool in pan on a wire rack 5 minutes. Remove from pan; cool completely on wire rack. Place cake on a serving plate; sift powdered sugar over cake immediately before serving. Makes 8 servings.

Chocolate-Covered Peanutty Bars

6 oz. semisweet or sweet chocolate
3 tablespoons butter or margarine
20 graham-cracker squares
1 (14-oz.) can sweetened condensed milk
3 tablespoons light corn syrup
1/4 cup crunchy peanut butter

1. Line bottom and sides of an 11" x 7" baking pan with foil, extending foil 2 inches above rim of pan all the way around.
2. Melt chocolate and 1 tablespoon butter or margarine in a small heavy saucepan over very low heat; stir until smooth. Spread 1/2 of chocolate mixture in bottom of foil-lined pan, covering bottom of pan completely. Reserve remaining chocolate mixture for topping.
3. Arrange 1/2 of graham crackers over chocolate, breaking crackers into halves and quarters to make them fit snugly. Set aside.
4. In a medium saucepan, combine remaining 2 tablespoons butter or margarine, condensed milk and corn syrup. Cook, stirring, until mixture comes to a boil. Boil 3 minutes, stirring constantly. Remove from heat; stir in peanut butter. Stir vigorously 1 minute or until mixture thickens. Pour over crackers; spread evenly.
5. Arrange remaining crackers over caramel filling, breaking crackers to fit. Press crackers down lightly. Spread reserved chocolate mixture over crackers. Refrigerate, uncovered, 1 hour or until chocolate is firm.
6. To serve, invert pan onto a flat surface. Peel off foil; cut cookies into 24 bars. Makes 24 cookies.

Chocolate-Fudge Bars

1/4 cup light corn syrup
10 tablespoons butter or margarine
6 oz. semisweet chocolate, coarsely chopped
28 graham-cracker squares, coarsely crushed
3/4 cup flaked or shredded coconut
1/4 cup chopped red candied cherries
1/3 cup raisins

1. Line an 8-inch-square baking pan with foil. Set aside.
2. In a large saucepan over low heat, combine corn syrup, butter or margarine and chocolate. Stir until mixture is smooth. Remove from heat.
3. Stir in cracker crumbs until combined. Fold in coconut, cherries and raisins. Pour mixture into lined pan; press down firmly with back of a wooden spoon. Cool to room temperature. Refrigerate 2 to 3 hours or until firm.
4. Remove from pan; place on a flat surface. Peel off foil; cut into bars. Refrigerate during hot weather. Makes 24 to 32 bars.

Chocolate-Topped Coconut Pyramids

Pyramids:
1 (14-oz.) can sweetened condensed milk
1 (12-oz.) pkg. flaked coconut (4 cups loosely packed)
2 oz. semisweet chocolate, finely chopped

To decorate:
3 oz. sweet or milk chocolate, chopped
Flaked coconut
Red candied cherries, quartered

---

1. Preheat oven to 375F (190C). Line 2 baking sheets with parchment paper.
2. In a large bowl, stir condensed milk, coconut and chocolate with a wooden spoon until combined.
3. Shape mixture into large walnut-sized balls. Place balls about 1-1/2 inches apart on lined baking sheets.
4. Bake in preheated oven 15 to 18 minutes or until golden brown. Cool on baking sheets on wire racks 5 minutes. Remove from baking sheets; cool completely on wire racks.
5. To decorate, melt chocolate in a small heavy saucepan over very low heat; stir until smooth. Let cool. Dip tops of coconut pyramids into melted chocolate. Decorate with coconut and cherries. Let stand until chocolate is set. Makes about 36.

Treasure Cups can also be used to serve individual helpings of Chunky-Fudge Ice Cream, page 13. For an elegant finale to a dinner party, serve Treasure Cups filled with a rich chocolate mousse, such as Rum & Raisin Mousse, page 32, topped with a dollop of whipped cream.

Chocolate Treasure Cups

8 oz. semisweet chocolate, chopped
6 double-foil cupcake cases, about 2-1/2 inches in diameter

Filling:
6 teaspoons raspberry jam or strawberry jam
1 (11-oz.) can mandarin-orange sections
1-1/2 cups sponge-cake crumbs
1 teaspoon unflavored gelatin powder

To decorate:
Red, green and yellow candied cherries, quartered

---

1. Melt chocolate in a small heavy saucepan over very low heat; stir until smooth. Let cool.
2. Spoon about 1 heaping tablespoon melted chocolate into bottom of 1 foil cupcake case. Spread chocolate over bottom and up side of case with back of spoon, covering inside of case completely. Place in muffin pan. Repeat with remaining chocolate and foil cases. Refrigerate 30 minutes or until firm.
3. Recoat insides of cases with remaining melted chocolate; refrigerate until firm.
4. To make filling, spoon 1 teaspoon jam into bottom of each chocolate cup.
5. Drain orange sections, reserving juice. Reserve 4 or 5 orange sections for decoration. Finely chop remaining sections. In a medium bowl, combine chopped orange sections and cake crumbs.
6. In a small saucepan, combine gelatin and reserved orange syrup. Stir well; let stand 3 minutes. Stir over low heat until gelatin dissolves; let cool. Stir cooled gelatin mixture into crumb mixture; stir until blended.
7. Spoon mixture into chocolate cups. Refrigerate 1 to 2 hours or until set.
8. To serve, carefully peel foil cases off chocolate cups, using tip of sharp knife to loosen foil from chocolate. Coarsely chop reserved orange sections. Decorate cups with candied cherries and chopped orange sections. Makes 6 servings.

Variation
Substitute 1 (8-ounce) can crushed pineapple for mandarin oranges. Make as directed above.

Chocolate & Honey Toffee

3/4 cup honey
1/3 cup firmly packed light-brown sugar
1/2 cup butter or margarine
2 teaspoons ground cinnamon
3 oz. semisweet or sweet chocolate, chopped

1. Butter an 8-inch-square pan.
2. In a medium saucepan over low heat, stir honey and brown sugar until sugar dissolves.

3. Stir in butter or margarine until melted. Increase heat; boil until mixture reaches soft-crack stage 270F to 290F (132C to 143C) on a candy thermometer. Remove from heat.
4. Stir in cinnamon until blended. Pour into buttered pan; let stand in a cool place until almost firm. Score into 32 (2" x 1") pieces. When cold, invert onto a flat surface; cut along scored lines.
5. Melt chocolate in a small heavy saucepan over very low heat; stir until smooth. Let cool.
6. Dip each piece of toffee halfway into cooled chocolate. Place on a sheet of waxed paper or foil; let stand until chocolate is set. Makes 32 pieces.

Clockwise from left: Chocolate-Topped Coconut Pyramids, Chocolate & Honey Toffee, Chocolate Treasure Cups

Barney Bee

1 recipe Quick Chocolate Cake, page 66
1 recipe Chocolate Buttercream, page 51
Chocolate sprinkles
5 oz. semisweet chocolate, chopped
1/4 cup light corn syrup
10 oz. white chocolate, chopped
Yellow food coloring
3 oz. marzipan
Powdered sugar

---

1. Preheat oven to 350F (175C). Grease an 8" x 4" loaf pan and a 3-cup heatproof bowl. Line bottom of bowl with a circle of waxed paper; grease paper.
2. Prepare Quick Chocolate Cake as directed on page 66. Pour batter into prepared pan and bowl, filling each about two-thirds full.
3. Bake both cakes at the same time. Position smaller cake near front of oven so it can be quickly removed when done. Bake in preheated oven 45 to 50 minutes for loaf cake and 50 to 60 minutes for bowl cake or until a wooden pick inserted in centers comes out clean. Cool in containers on wire racks 5 minutes. Invert onto wire racks; remove containers and paper. Cool completely on wire racks.
4. Prepare Chocolate Buttercream as directed on page 51.
5. Cut cooled loaf cake in half lengthwise; sandwich together with a little buttercream. Place cake on a flat surface. Cut bowl cake from top to bottom making 1 piece two-thirds of cake. Spread buttercream over cut edge of large piece of cake; press against 1 end of loaf cake. Spread buttercream over cut edge of small piece of cake; press against opposite end of loaf cake. Trim sides even with loaf cake.
6. Set aside 1 tablespoon buttercream. Spread remaining buttercream over top and sides of cake, covering cake completely. Press chocolate sprinkles around large end of cake to make the head. Place cake on a decorative 14-inch-square cake board.
7. Melt 4 ounces semisweet chocolate in a small heavy saucepan over very low heat; stir until smooth. Stir in 2 tablespoons corn syrup. Pour chocolate mixture onto a small baking sheet. Refrigerate 25 minutes or until set. Remove chocolate from baking sheet with a dough scraper. On a flat surface, knead vigorously 3 minutes. Shape into a flattened ball; wrap in plastic wrap. Let stand at room temperature 40 minutes. Divide into 2 equal pieces; knead each piece vigorously 1 minute. Flatten each piece. Turn pasta machine to widest setting; pass each piece of chocolate through machine 3 times, folding chocolate into thirds before running through machine. Adjust machine to next widest setting; run chocolate through without folding. Place chocolate strips on a flat surface; cut into 4 ribbons, each 1 inch wide and 9 inches long.
8. To make 4 yellow ribbons, melt 4 ounces white chocolate in a small heavy saucepan over very low heat; stir until smooth. Stir in remaining 2 tablespoons corn syrup and a few drops yellow food coloring. Follow chilling, rolling and cutting directions above for making chocolate ribbons.

Barney Bee

9. Starting behind head, place alternate strips of yellow and chocolate ribbons over body. Gather dark chocolate scraps; knead until smooth. Flatten and roll out with a rolling pin. Place over tail at end of body. Trim edges of yellow and chocolate ribbons even with bottom of cake, if necessary.
10. Draw 2 wings on a sheet of parchment paper, each about 7 inches long and 3 inches wide. Melt remaining 6 ounces white chocolate in a small heavy saucepan over very low heat; stir until smooth. Pour white chocolate inside wing outlines; spread evenly. Let stand until completely set. Melt remaining 1 ounce semisweet chocolate in a small heavy saucepan over very low heat; stir until smooth. Spoon into a pastry bag fitted with a small plain writing tip. Pipe narrow chocolate lines on wings to represent veins. Let stand until chocolate is completely set.
11. Place marzipan in a small bowl; knead in a few drops of yellow food coloring. Knead until marzipan is smooth. Add powdered sugar if marzipan is too soft to shape. Divide marzipan into 2 pieces, making 1 piece 2/3 of marzipan. Cut large piece of marzipan into 6 equal pieces. Roll out each piece with palm of your hand to make 6 ropes, each 6 inches long. Dab a little buttercream at 1 end of each rope. Press onto body of wasp for legs, bending each stick; see photo. Cut remaining piece of marzipan into 5 pieces. Use 2 small pieces to make eyes; attach to head with buttercream. Roll 1 piece into a thin stick for mouth; attach to face with buttercream. Shape remaining 2 pieces of marzipan around 2 small wooden picks, leaving 1/4 of pick uncovered; insert uncovered part into head for antennae.
12. Cut slit on each side of body for inserting wings. Carefully remove wings from paper. Gently insert 1 white-chocolate wing into each slit. Support backs of wings with popsicle sticks. Refrigerate until served. Remove antennae before serving to prevent anyone eating wooden picks by mistake. Makes 8 to 10 servings.

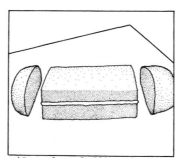

1/Cut cake in half lengthwise; sandwich together with a little buttercream.

2/Starting behind head, place alternate strips of yellow and chocolate ribbons over body.

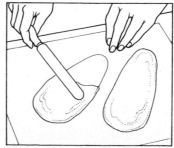

3/Pour white chocolate over wing outlines; spread evenly.

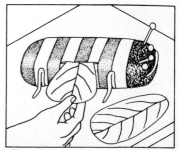

4/Gently insert 1 white-chocolate wing into each slit.

Ozzy Owl

1 recipe Quick Chocolate Cake, page 66
1 recipe Chocolate Buttercream, page 51
1 sugar ice-cream cone
5 oz. marzipan
Red and green food coloring
1 oz. white chocolate
8 oz. dark semisweet- or sweet-chocolate buttons

---

1. Preheat oven to 350F (175C). Grease a 3-cup heatproof bowl and a 6-cup heatproof bowl. Line bottoms of bowls with waxed paper; grease paper. Prepare Quick Chocolate Cake as directed on page 66. Pour 2/3 of batter into prepared large bowl and remaining batter into prepared small bowl.

2. Bake both cakes at the same time. Position smaller cake near front of oven so it can be quickly removed when done. Bake small bowl in preheated oven 40 to 45 minutes and large bowl 1 hour 10 minutes or until a wooden pick inserted in centers comes out clean. Cool in bowls on wire racks 5 minutes. Invert on wire racks; remove bowls and paper. Cool completely on wire racks.

3. Prepare Chocolate Buttercream as directed on page 51. Cut both cakes in half horizontally. Sandwich layers together with a little buttercream. Place large cake, flat-side down, on a cake board. Spread a little buttercream on top; place small cake, flat-side down, on top. Trim sides of cakes as needed to make edges smooth and even. Set aside about 1/3 cup buttercream. Spread remaining buttercream around side and over top of cake, covering cake completely.

4. Cut ice-cream cone about 2 inches from tip, discarding tip. With kitchen scissors, cut cone in half lengthwise. Trim halves with a sharp knife or scissors to make ears for owl. Spread buttercream over ears; place ears on top of cake.

5. Place marzipan in a small bowl; add a few drops of red and green food coloring. Knead until marzipan is an even shade of brown. Remove a small piece of marzipan; shape into a small hooked beak. Use about 1/4 of remaining marzipan to make 2 feet with 3 claws each. Divide remaining marzipan in half; shape into 2 ovals for wings. Press wings onto sides of lower part of owl; curve wings around body, leaving small space between wings and body. Spread with buttercream.

6. Melt white chocolate in a small heavy saucepan over very low heat; stir until smooth. Draw 2 small oval egg-size shapes on a sheet of waxed paper. Spread melted white chocolate inside ovals. Place a chocolate button on each oval for eyes. Let stand until completely set. Attach ovals to head of owl with a dab of buttercream.

7. Place a row of chocolate buttons around bottom edge of owl; repeat rows of buttons, slightly overlapping, until body and head of owl is completely covered. Do not cover face. Press beak between eyes; place feet at bottom of owl. Makes 8 to 10 servings.

Thomas Toad

1 recipe Quick Chocolate Cake, page 66
1 recipe Chocolate Buttercream, page 51
About 3/4 cup chocolate sprinkles
2 chocolate-covered marshmallow cookies
5 small round white candies
Red licorice rope
1/2 cup flaked coconut
Blue, green and yellow food coloring
4 oz. marzipan

---

1. Preheat oven to 350F (175C). Grease a 3-cup heatproof bowl and a 6-cup heatproof bowl. Line bottoms of bowls with waxed paper; grease paper. Prepare Quick Chocolate Cake as directed on page 66. Pour 2/3 of batter into prepared large bowl and remaining batter into prepared small bowl.

2. Bake both cakes at the same time. Position smaller cake near front of oven so it can be quickly removed when done. Bake small bowl in preheated oven 40 to 45 minutes and large bowl 1 hour 10 minutes or until a wooden pick inserted in centers comes out clean. Cool in bowls on wire racks 5 minutes. Invert on wire racks; remove bowls and paper. Cool completely on wire racks.

3. Prepare Chocolate Buttercream as directed on page 51. Cut both cakes in half horizontally. Sandwich layers together with a little buttercream. Place large cake, flat-side down, on a cake board. Spread a little buttercream on top; place small cake, flat-side down, on top. Trim sides of cakes as needed to make edges smooth and even. Set aside about 1/3 cup buttercream. Spread remaining buttercream around side and over top of cake, covering cake completely.

4. Spread some of reserved buttercream on bottom of marshmallow cookies; place cookies on top of cake to make eyes. Spread backs of 2 white candies with some of reserved buttercream; arrange center of cookies to make eyes. Place cake on a 10-inch-round cake board.

5. Cut out a half-moon wedge halfway down cake beneath eyes to make mouth. Remove wedge; place a small piece of red licorice across bottom of mouth.

6. In a small bowl, toss coconut with a few drops blue food coloring. Spread coconut on cake board around toad.

7. Divide marzipan into 2 pieces, making 1 piece 2/3 of marzipan. In a small bowl, knead a few drops green food coloring into large piece of marzipan; knead until smooth. In a small bowl, knead yellow food coloring into small piece of marzipan. Divide green marzipan into 9 small pieces; flatten each piece into a small circle. Arrange circles on top of coconut in groups of 3 to make 3 lily pads.

8. Divide yellow marzipan in thirds. Flatten into 3 circles. Snip out small triangles around edge of each circle to make water lilies. Curve snipped edges up slightly; place on lily pads. Place white candy in center of each water lily. See variation for Chocolate-Frog Pond, opposite page, for remaining decorations. Makes 8 to 10 servings.

Chocolate-Frog Pond

1 (6-oz.) pkg. lime-flavored gelatin
1/4 cup whipping cream, whipped
About 12 miniature chocolate eggs, unwrapped
Colored candy flowers
1 (2-oz.) strip of angelica

1. Prepare gelatin as directed on package. Pour into a large shallow dish. Refrigerate until firm.

2. Spoon whipped cream into a pastry bag fitted with a fine writing tip. Pipe dots for eyes and a strip for a mouth on 1 end of each egg. Stick onto gelatin with a dollop of whipped cream.
3. Place candy flowers in groups on firm gelatin.
4. Cut angelica into fine strips; stick into gelatin for reeds. Chill before serving. Makes 6 to 8 servings.

Variation
Use large creme-filled chocolate eggs. Use candied-cherry halves for eyes and chocolate buttons for feet.

Top to bottom: Ozzy Owl, Chocolate-Frog Pond, Thomas Toad

Top to bottom: Choc Around the Clock, Meringue Cookies

Quick Chocolate Cake

3/4 cup butter or margarine, room temperature
1-1/4 cups sugar
4 eggs
1 teaspoon vanilla extract
1-1/2 cups all-purpose flour
1/4 cup unsweetened cocoa powder
1 teaspoon baking powder
1/4 teaspoon baking soda
1/2 teaspoon salt
1/3 cup milk

1. Preheat oven to 350F (175C). Grease and flour 2 (8-inch) round cake pans.
2. In a medium bowl, beat butter or margarine and sugar until light and fluffy. Beat in eggs and vanilla until blended.
3. Sift flour, cocoa, baking powder, baking soda and salt into a medium bowl. Add to egg mixture alternately with milk; beat until blended. Beat 1 minute with an electric mixer at medium speed, scraping side of bowl occasionally. Pour batter into prepared pans; smooth tops.
4. Bake in preheated oven 30 to 35 minutes or until a wooden pick inserted in center comes out clean. Cool in pans on wire racks 5 minutes. Remove from pans; cool completely on wire racks. Fill and frost as desired. Makes 6 to 8 servings.

Choc Around the Clock

2 cups self-rising flour
1/2 cup unsweetened cocoa powder
1/4 cup cornstarch
1-1/2 cups sugar
4 eggs, separated
3/4 cup vegetable oil
1 cup water

To decorate:
1 recipe Chocolate Buttercream, page 51
About 60 chocolate-covered finger cookies
1 cup powdered sugar, sifted
1 tablespoon warm water
2 chocolate-covered marshmallow cookies
Meringue Cookies, opposite, if desired

1. Preheat oven to 375F (190C). Grease 3 (9-inch) square baking pans.
2. Sift flour, cocoa and cornstarch into a large bowl; stir in sugar until blended. In a small bowl, beat egg yolks, oil and water until blended. Add to flour mixture; beat with an electric mixer at low speed until thoroughly blended, scraping down side of bowl occasionally.
3. In a medium bowl, beat egg whites until stiff but not dry. Fold beaten egg whites into chocolate mixture. Divide batter equally among greased pans; smooth tops.
4. Bake in preheated oven 20 to 25 minutes or until centers spring back when lightly pressed. Cool in pans on wire racks 5 minutes. Remove from pans; cool completely on wire racks.
5. Prepare Chocolate Buttercream as directed on page 51. Set aside 1/3 of buttercream for decoration. Place 1 cake layer on a flat surface; spread with a thin layer of buttercream. Top with a second layer; spread with buttercream. Place third layer on top. Spread remaining buttercream around sides of cake. Press chocolate fingers into buttercream around sides.
6. Position cake at center of top edge of a 14-inch-square white cake board.
7. Mark a 7-inch circle in center of cake with a knife tip. In a small bowl, blend powdered sugar and water until mixture is smooth. Spread inside marked circle; let stand until completely set.
8. Spoon all but 2 tablespoons reserved buttercream into a pastry bag fitted with a small open-star tip. Pipe buttercream in small stars around edge of circle and over remaining top of cake. If desired, pipe additional buttercream stars around edge of cake board.
9. Spoon remaining buttercream into a small pastry bag fitted with a small plain writing tip. Pipe numbers and hands on white circle for face of clock and 2 chains of tiny circles below clock, making 1 chain slightly longer than other. Place marshmallow cookie at bottom of each chain. Decorate board with fanciful Meringue Cookies, opposite, if desired. Makes 9 to 12 servings.

Meringue Cookies

4 egg whites
1/2 cup sugar
1 cup powdered sugar
1/4 cup unsweetened cocoa powder

To decorate:
Whole cloves
Flaked almonds
Slivered almonds

1. Preheat oven to 300F (150C). Line baking sheets with parchment paper.
2. In a medium bowl, beat egg whites until soft peaks form. Beat in sugars until stiff and glossy. Sift cocoa over meringue; fold in.
3. Spoon meringue into a pastry bag fitted with a coupling. Using the appropriate tip suggested below, pipe shapes on paper-lined baking sheets; see directions below.
4. Bake meringues in preheated oven about 45 minutes to 1 hour, depending on size, or until completely dried out. Cool on baking sheets on wire racks. Carefully remove cooled meringues from paper. Meringue shapes can be stored up to 2 weeks in an airtight container at room temperature. Makes 50 to 70 cookies depending on size.

Shaping Instructions:
Snails: Using a 1/2-inch plain tip, pipe a short straight length of meringue to form a head; from straight line, make a circle. Continue piping in a spiral to form shell. Insert 2 whole cloves in head to make feelers.
Mice: Using a 1/2-inch plain tip, pipe about 1 inch of meringue. Then pipe a large bulb of meringue back over top, releasing pressure into a long-drawn-out point. At pointed end, insert 2 whole cloves into meringue for eyes and 2 almonds flakes for ears.
Hedgehogs: Using a 3/4-inch star tip, pipe about 1 inch of meringue. Then pipe back over this, releasing pressure to form a sharp point. Insert 2 whole cloves into pointed end of meringue to form eyes; insert halved slivered almonds all over back to form spines.
Stars: Using a 3/4-inch star tip, hold bag vertically; squeeze out a star of meringue. Release pressure quickly to avoid a long point.
Rosettes: Using a 3/4-inch star or rosette tip, pipe meringue in a circle; finish by bringing tip into center of circle. Release quickly.

Chocolate Pavlova

AUSTRALIA

Meringue:
3 egg whites
1 cup superfine sugar
1/4 cup unsweetened cocoa powder
2 tablespoons cornstarch
1 teaspoon lemon juice or white vinegar

Filling:
1/2 pint whipping cream (1 cup)
1 teaspoon vanilla extract
2 tablespoons powdered sugar
2 oz. semisweet chocolate, grated
1 pint fresh strawberries, washed, hulled (2 cups)
Powdered sugar

Pavlova, an Australian dessert, was created in honor of Mme. Pavlova, the famous ballerina. The center of the meringue is hollowed out slightly before baking. The cooled pavlova is usually filled with whipped cream and fruit.

1. Preheat oven to 300F (150C). Line a baking sheet with parchment paper. Draw an 8-inch circle on parchment paper.
2. In a large bowl, beat egg whites until stiff peaks form. Beat in superfine sugar, 1 tablespoon at a time, until meringue is stiff and glossy.
3. Sift cocoa and cornstarch over meringue; fold into meringue with lemon juice or vinegar.
4. Spoon meringue inside circle on lined baking sheet. Spread evenly; hollow out center slightly, pushing meringue toward edge of circle.
5. Bake in preheated oven 1 hour 30 minutes to 2 hours or until meringue is crisp on the outside. Cool on baking sheet on a wire rack 15 minutes. Carefully peel off lining paper; cool completely on wire rack.
6. To make filling, in a medium bowl, beat cream until soft peaks form. Beat in vanilla and powdered sugar. Fold in chocolate. Spoon chocolate-cream mixture into center of cooled meringue; spread to edge of hollowed-out center. Arrange strawberries on top of cream mixture. Refrigerate until served. Sift powdered sugar over strawberries immediately before serving. Fill and serve meringue the same day. Makes 4 to 6 servings.

Viennese Chocolate Spritz

AUSTRIA

Cookies:
2 oz. unsweetened chocolate
1 cup butter or margarine, room temperature
1 cup sugar
1 teaspoon vanilla extract
1/4 teaspoon salt
2 egg yolks
2-1/2 cups sifted all-purpose flour

To decorate:
6 oz. semisweet chocolate, melted, cooled
Powdered sugar

1. Preheat oven to 375F (190C). To make cookies, melt chocolate in a small heavy saucepan over very low heat; stir until smooth. Let cool.
2. In a medium bowl, beat butter or margarine and sugar until light and fluffy. Beat in vanilla, salt and egg yolks until blended.
3. Beat in cooled chocolate. Gradually stir in flour with a wooden spoon until thoroughly combined.
4. Spoon dough into a large pastry bag fitted with a 3/4-inch star tip. Pipe out dough in S shapes about 1 inch apart on ungreased baking sheets.
5. Bake in preheated oven 8 to 10 minutes or until firm when lightly pressed. Remove from baking sheets; cool completely on wire racks.
6. To decorate, dip 1 end of cooled cookies into chocolate. Place on foil or waxed paper; let stand until chocolate is set. Sift powdered sugar over other ends of cookies. Makes 54 to 60 cookies.

Top to bottom: Chocolate Pavlova, Viennese Chocolate Spritz

Creole Cake

CARIBBEAN

1/3 cup dried apricots, finely chopped
1/4 cup dark rum
1 recipe Cocoa Layer Cake, page 51
1 cup flaked coconut
4 oz. semisweet chocolate, chopped
1 tablespoon butter or margarine
1 tablespoon instant coffee powder
2 tablespoons light-brown sugar
1/4 cup boiling water
1/4 cup apricot jam
1-1/2 cups whipping cream
2 tablespoons powdered sugar

To decorate:
Chocolate bark, page 8

1. In a medium bowl, combine apricots and rum. Let stand at room temperature 4 hours.
2. Preheat oven to 350F (175C). Grease and flour 2 (8-inch) square baking pans.
3. Prepare Cocoa Layer Cake as directed on page 51, folding 2/3 cup coconut into batter. Pour batter into prepared pans.

4. Bake in preheated oven 25 to 30 minutes or until centers spring back when lightly pressed. Cool in pans on wire racks 5 minutes. Remove from pans; cool completely on wire racks.
5. Melt chocolate and butter or margarine in a small heavy saucepan over very low heat; stir until smooth. Let cool. Stir in remaining 1/3 cup coconut.
6. In a medium bowl, blend coffee, brown sugar and boiling water until smooth.
7. Finely crumble 1 cake layer. Fold 1/3 of cake crumbs into apricot-rum mixture, 1/3 into chocolate-coconut mixture and remaining 1/3 into coffee mixture.
8. Cut remaining layer in half horizontally. Place 1/2 of layer on a serving plate; spread with 2 tablespoons apricot jam. Spread crumb-apricot mixture over jam; smooth top. Spread crumb-chocolate mixture over apricot mixture; smooth top. Spread crumb-coffee mixture over chocolate mixture; smooth top. Spread cut side of second half with remaining 2 tablespoons apricot jam. Place layer, jam-side down, on top of last filling layer; press down lightly.
9. In a medium bowl, beat cream until soft peaks form. Beat in powdered sugar. Spread whipped-cream mixture around sides and over top of cake, covering completely. Decorate cake with chocolate bark. Refrigerate until served. Makes 9 servings.

Left to right: Creole Cake, Danish Spice Cake, Chocolate Posset

Danish Spice Cake

DENMARK

Cake:
3/4 cup butter or margarine
1 cup sugar
1 egg
1 cup all-purpose flour
1/4 cup unsweetened cocoa powder
2 teaspoons ground allspice

Topping:
2 oz. semisweet chocolate, chopped
1/4 cup chopped, toasted, blanched almonds

Filling:
1-1/2 cups whipping cream
1 teaspoon vanilla extract
3 tablespoons powdered sugar
3/4 cup chopped, toasted, blanched almonds

1. Cut out 6 (8- or 9-inch) parchment-paper circles. Set 4 parchment circles aside. Turn 2 (8- or 9-inch) round cake pans upside down; grease outside bottom surface. Place 1 parchment circle on greased surface of each pan. Lightly grease parchment paper. Set aside.
2. Preheat oven to 375F (190C).
3. In a medium bowl, beat butter or margarine and sugar until light and fluffy. Beat in egg until blended.
4. Sift flour, cocoa and allspice over egg mixture; fold in.
5. Spread about 1/3 cup mixture on each paper-covered cake pan, starting from center and spreading mixture toward edge.
6. Bake in preheated oven 10 minutes. Cool layers on pans 2 minutes. Slide off pan carefully; cool completely on wire racks. Do not remove lining paper. Prepare pans again; repeat with remaining mixture 2 more times to make a total of 6 layers. Layers are very fragile; do not stack.
7. To make topping, melt chocolate in a small saucepan over low heat; stir until smooth. Peel lining paper off 1 layer; place on a flat surface. Spread melted chocolate over layer; sprinkle with almonds. Let stand until set.
8. To make filling, in a medium bowl, beat cream until soft peaks form. Beat in vanilla and powdered sugar. Fold in almonds. Carefully peel lining paper off remaining 5 layers. Place 1 layer on a serving plate; spread with a thin layer of cream mixture. Top with second layer; spread with cream mixture. Repeat with remaining layers and cream mixture, ending with layer of cream mixture. Place chocolate-covered layer on top. Refrigerate until served. Makes 8 to 10 servings.

Chocolate Posset

ENGLAND

1 pint whipping cream (2 cups)
6 tablespoons chocolate-flavored drink mix
3 tablespoons sugar
1 teaspoon ground cinnamon
6 to 8 tablespoons gin
3 egg whites

To decorate:
Chocolate curls, page 7

1. In a large bowl, beat cream until soft peaks form. Beat in drink mix, sugar and cinnamon until blended. Do not overbeat; mixture should not be stiff.
2. Stir in gin, 1 tablespoon at a time, to taste.
3. In a medium bowl, beat egg whites until stiff but not dry. Fold beaten egg whites into chocolate-cream mixture. Refrigerate several hours or overnight.
4. To serve, whisk chilled mixture until thick and fluffy. Spoon into wine glasses or individual dessert dishes. Decorate with chocolate curls. Makes 6 to 8 servings.

Chocolate Bakewell Tart
ENGLAND

Pastry:
1-1/2 cups all-purpose flour
1/4 teaspoon salt
1/4 cup butter or margarine
1/4 cup vegetable shortening
1 egg yolk
2 to 3 tablespoons iced water

Filling:
3 tablespoons seedless raspberry jam
1/3 cup butter or margarine, room temperature
1/2 cup sugar
2 eggs
1 teaspoon almond extract
2 tablespoons unsweetened cocoa powder
1/3 cup finely ground almonds
1/3 cup sponge-cake crumbs
1/4 cup sliced almonds

1. To make pastry, in a medium bowl, combine flour and salt. With a pastry blender or 2 knives, cut in butter or margarine and shortening until mixture resembles coarse crumbs. In a small bowl, beat egg yolk and 2 tablespoons water until blended; sprinkle over flour mixture. Stir with a fork until mixture binds together, adding more water if necessary. Shape into a flattened ball. Wrap in waxed paper; refrigerate 30 minutes.
2. On a lightly floured surface, roll out pastry to a 13" x 9" rectangle. Use pastry to line an 11" x 7" baking pan, pressing pastry about 1 inch up sides of pan. Lightly prick bottom of pastry with a fork.
3. Preheat oven to 350F (175C). To make filling, spread jam over pastry. In a medium bowl, beat butter or margarine and sugar until creamy. Beat in eggs and almond extract until blended. Sift cocoa into a small bowl; stir in grounds almonds. Fold cocoa mixture and cake crumbs into egg mixture. Spread mixture evenly over jam. Sprinkle with sliced almonds.
4. Bake in preheated oven 30 to 40 minutes or until center is slightly firm when lightly pressed. Cool completely in pan on a wire rack. Cut into rectangles to serve. Makes 8 to 10 servings.

Truffles
FRANCE

1 tablespoon instant coffee powder
2 tablespoons boiling water
8 oz. semisweet chocolate, chopped
1/2 cup butter or margarine, cubed
2 tablespoons dark rum
Powdered sugar
Chocolate sprinkles

Truffles improve with standing. Make them at least 2 to 3 days before serving.

1. In top of a double boiler set over a pan of simmering water, dissolve coffee in boiling water. Add chocolate; stir until smooth. Remove top of double boiler from heat. With a wooden spoon, gradually beat in butter or margarine until melted and mixture is smooth and thick. Stir in rum until blended.
2. Pour mixture into a medium bowl; refrigerate 2 to 3 hours or until firm. Place chocolate sprinkles in a wide shallow dish. Dust your hands with powdered sugar. Using your sugar-coated hands, roll chocolate mixture into walnut-sized balls.
3. Roll truffles in sprinkles to coat completely; place in small paper cases. Refrigerate until served. Makes about 24 truffles.

Left to right: Truffles, Chocolate Bakewell Tart, Finnish Gâteau

Finnish Gâteau

FINLAND

1 recipe cake layers for Ganache Torte, page 39

Filling:
2 tablespoons cornstarch
1/3 cup sugar
1-1/4 cups milk
2 egg yolks, beaten
1 teaspoon vanilla extract
1 tablespoon butter or margarine, room temperature
1 cup chunk-style applesauce

Icing:
1-1/2 cups sugar
2/3 cup half and half
2 tablespoons light corn syrup
2 oz. unsweetened chocolate, chopped
2 tablespoons butter or margarine
About 1/2 cup chopped, toasted, blanched almonds

1. Prepare and bake cake layers through step 4 as directed on page 39. Cut each layer in half as directed.
2. To make filling, in a medium saucepan, combine cornstarch and sugar. Gradually stir in milk. Cook over low heat, stirring, until mixture thickens and comes to a boil. Remove from heat.
3. Stir 1/4 cup hot milk mixture into egg yolks. Return mixture to pan; stir well. Cook, stirring, until mixture is thickened. Do not boil. Pour into a medium bowl. Stir in vanilla and butter or margarine until butter or margarine melts. Cover surface of custard with a sheet of waxed paper to prevent a skin from forming. Refrigerate 2 to 3 hours or until completely chilled.
4. Place 1 cake layer on a serving plate; spread with 1/2 of chilled custard. Top with second layer; spread with applesauce. Top with third layer; spread with remaining custard. Top with fourth layer; lightly press down on cake.
5. To make icing, in a medium saucepan over medium heat, combine sugar, half and half, corn syrup and chocolate. Cook, stirring, until chocolate melts and sugar dissolves. Boil rapidly, without stirring, to soft-ball stage 234F (113C) on a candy thermometer. Remove from heat; stir in butter or margarine. Cool to lukewarm.
6. Beat cooled icing with a wooden spoon until icing thickens and loses its gloss. Spread icing over side and top of cake with a flat spatula. Press almonds lightly into icing around side of cake. Makes 6 to 8 servings.

Bûche de Noël

FRANCE

Cake:
4 eggs, separated
1/2 cup granulated sugar
1/2 teaspoon vanilla extract
1/2 cup sifted cake flour
1/4 cup unsweetened cocoa powder
1/2 teaspoon salt
Powdered sugar

Filling & Frosting:
Double recipe Chocolate Buttercream, page 51
1 tablespoon instant coffee powder
2 tablespoons boiling water

To decorate:
Red and green candied cherries
Powdered sugar

1. Preheat oven to 400F (205C). Grease a 15" x 10" jelly-roll pan. Line bottom of pan with waxed paper; grease paper.

2. To make cake, in a medium bowl, beat egg yolks until creamy. Beat in granulated sugar until thick and lemon-colored. Beat in vanilla. Sift flour, cocoa and salt over egg-yolk mixture; fold in.
3. In a medium bowl, beat egg whites until stiff but not dry. Fold beaten egg whites into egg-yolk mixture. Spread mixture in prepared pan; smooth top.
4. Bake in preheated oven 12 to 15 minutes or until center springs back when lightly pressed.
5. Sift powdered sugar over a clean towel; invert cake onto sugared towel. Peel off lining paper; trim crusty edges. Starting from short end, roll up cake in towel. Cool completely on a wire rack.
6. To make filling, prepare buttercream as directed on page 51, omitting half and half. In a small bowl, dissolve coffee in boiling water. Cool slightly. Beat cooled coffee into buttercream until blended.
7. Unroll cooled cake; spread 1/2 of buttercream over cake to within 1/2 inch of edges. Reroll cake, without towel; place, seam-side down, on a serving plate. Completely cover cake with remaining buttercream. Draw prongs of a fork over icing to create a bark effect. Decorate with candied cherries. Refrigerate until served. Sift powdered sugar over roll immediately before serving. Makes 10 to 12 servings.

Left to right: Bûche de Noël, Piped Mocha Truffles, Pacific Gold

Piped Mocha Truffles

FRANCE

Chocolate Cases:
4 oz. semisweet chocolate, chopped
16 foil petits-four cases

Filling:
1 teaspoon instant coffee powder
1 tablespoon hot water
5 oz. semisweet or sweet chocolate, chopped
2 tablespoons whipping cream
1/4 cup butter or margarine, cubed
2 egg yolks, beaten
1 to 2 tablespoons dark rum

To decorate:
Crystallized candy violets

1. To make chocolate cases, melt chocolate in a small heavy saucepan over very low heat; stir until smooth. Cool slightly.

2. Spoon about 1 teaspoon melted chocolate into each foil case. Spread chocolate over bottom and up side of cases with back of spoon or your fingertip, covering insides completely. Place on a baking sheet; refrigerate about 20 minutes or until chocolate is completely set. Recoat inside of cases with remaining melted chocolate; let stand until chocolate is set.

3. Peel foil cases off chocolate cups carefully, using a knife tip to loosen chocolate from foil.

4. To make filling, in top of a double boiler set over a pan of simmering water, dissolve coffee in boiling water. Add chocolate; stir until smooth. Stir in cream until mixture is smooth and thickened. Remove top of double boiler from heat.

5. Gradually beat in butter or margarine, a little at a time, beating until butter or margarine melts. Beat in egg yolks and rum until thoroughly blended. Refrigerate about 30 minutes or until mixture is completely cool and thickened. Mixture should still be soft enough to pipe.

6. Spoon chocolate filling into a pastry bag fitted with a medium star tip; pipe filling into chocolate cups. Decorate with violets. Makes 16 truffles.

Pacific Gold

PACIFIC

1/2 recipe Chocolate-Cookie Ice Cream, page 13, or
    other ice cream
1 fresh small or medium pineapple
2 egg whites
1/2 cup sugar
1/2 teaspoon vanilla extract

1. Make and freeze ice cream according to directions on page 13.

2. Preheat oven to 475F (220C). Carefully cut a thin slice from top and bottom of pineapple. Reserve top; cut away any peel from around leaves. Peel pineapple; with a small knife or end of a vegetable peeler, remove eyes.

3. Cut pineapple into 4 to 6 slices; cut out center core.

4. Soften ice cream slightly. Reassemble pineapple, placing ice cream between each slice and in center hole. Place in a baking pan; freeze while preparing meringue.

5. In a medium bowl, beat egg whites until soft peaks form. Gradually beat in sugar, beating until meringue is stiff and glossy. Beat in vanilla.

6. Spoon meringue into a large piping bag fitted with a 3/4-inch star tip; pipe stars over chilled pineapple, completely covering pineapple down to baking pan.

7. Bake in a preheated oven about 3 minutes or until meringue tips are lightly browned.

8. Insert reserved leaves into position on top of meringue-covered pineapple. Serve immediately. Makes 4 to 6 servings.

Left to right: Russian Cake, Chocolate-Topped Shortbread, Mazariner

Russian Cake

RUSSIA

1 (10-3/4-oz.) pkg. frozen pound cake, thawed
5 tablespoons sweet sherry
1/4 cup raspberry jam or strawberry jam
3 tablespoons red-currant jelly
1 (7-oz.) pkg. marzipan
4 oz. semisweet chocolate, chopped
1 tablespoon butter or margarine

1. Remove cake from foil pan. Carefully wash and dry pan. Grease clean pan.
2. Cut cake horizontally into 3 layers. Place bottom layer in greased pan; sprinkle with 2 tablespoons sherry. Spread with 2 tablespoons jam; top with middle layer. Sprinkle with 2 tablespoons sherry; spread with remaining jam. Top with top layer; sprinkle with remaining 1 tablespoon sherry.

3. Place a sheet of waxed paper over cake; press down gently. Place a similar-sized loaf pan on top of cake; fill 1/3 full of pie weights or dried beans. Refrigerate overnight.
4. In a small saucepan over low heat, melt jelly; let cool. Remove weighted pan and waxed paper from cake. Invert cake onto a flat surface. Remove pan. Brush top and sides of cake with cooled jelly.
5. Roll out marzipan between 2 sheets of waxed paper to a rectangle large enough to cover top and sides of cake. Peel off 1 sheet of waxed paper; place marzipan over cake, covering cake completely. Peel off waxed paper. Press marzipan around cake; trim bottom edges.
6. Melt chocolate and butter or margarine in a small heavy saucepan over very low heat; stir until smooth. Let cool.
7. Spread cooled chocolate mixture over top and around sides of marzipan-covered cake, covering completely. Let stand until chocolate is set. Place cake on a serving plate; refrigerate until served. Makes 6 to 8 servings.

1. Preheat oven to 325F (165C). Grease an 8-inch-square baking pan. Line pan with waxed paper; grease paper.
2. To make shortbread, in a medium bowl, beat butter or margarine and sugar until light and fluffy. Stir in ground almonds and mixed fruit, if desired. Stir in flour to make a soft dough. Knead dough in bowl 8 to 10 strokes or until smooth. Press dough into prepared pan; smooth top.
3. Bake in preheated oven 30 to 35 minutes or until golden. Cool in pan on a wire rack 10 minutes. Remove from pan; peel off lining paper. Cool completely on wire rack. When cooled, return shortbread to pan.
4. To make icing, in a small saucepan over low heat, combine butter or margarine, milk and granulated sugar. Cook, stirring, until butter or margarine melts. Bring mixture to a boil; remove from heat. Sift cocoa and powdered sugar into a medium bowl. Beat in hot milk mixture until icing is stiff and completely cool. Spread icing over shortbread in pan. Make wavy lines in icing with prongs of a fork. Let stand until icing is set. Cut into bars; remove from pan. Makes 14 to 16 bars.

Mazariner
SWEDEN

Double recipe of pastry for Chocolate Chiffon Pie,
    page 28
1/4 cup butter or margarine, room temperature
1/2 cup sugar
1 egg
1/3 cup almonds, ground
Few drops almond extract
Green food coloring
4 oz. semisweet chocolate, broken into pieces
About 12 blanched almonds, toasted

1. Preheat oven to 350F (175C). Prepare pastry through step 1 as directed on page 28. On a lightly floured surface, roll out pastry to about 1/4 inch thick; cut out 12 (5-inch) circles. Use pastry to line 12 (3-inch) tart pans. Prick pastry with a fork.
2. In a medium bowl, beat butter or margarine and sugar until light and fluffy. Beat in egg. Carefully fold in ground almonds, almond extract to taste and enough green food coloring to make a pastel green. Fill each tart two-thirds full.
3. Bake in preheated oven about 15 minutes or until filling puffs. Cool on a wire rack.
4. Melt chocolate in a small heavy saucepan over very low heat; stir until smooth. Spread melted chocolate over cooled tarts. Place an almond on each tart; let stand until chocolate is set. Make 12 tarts.

Chocolate-Topped Shortbread
SCOTLAND

Shortbread:
1/2 cup butter or margarine, room temperature
1/2 cup sugar
1/4 cup finely ground blanched almonds
1/4 cup candied mixed fruit, if desired
1 cup all-purpose flour

Icing:
3 tablespoons butter or margarine
2 tablespoons milk
2 tablespoons granulated sugar
2 tablespoons unsweetened cocoa powder
1-1/2 cups powdered sugar

Chocolate-Muesli Bars

SWITZERLAND

Bars:
1/3 cup honey
1/2 cup butter or margarine
1/3 cup firmly packed light-brown sugar
1-3/4 cups muesli, see box below
1/3 cup raisins or semisweet chocolate pieces
1/3 cup chopped almonds

Topping:
4 oz. semisweet chocolate, chopped
1 tablespoon butter or margarine

---

1. Preheat oven to 350F (175C). Grease an 8-inch-square baking pan. Line pan with foil; grease foil.
2. In a large saucepan over low heat, combine honey, butter or margarine and brown sugar. Cook, stirring, until butter or margarine and sugar are melted. Remove from heat. Stir in muesli, raisins or chocolate pieces and nuts until distributed. Press mixture evenly into bottom of prepared pan.
3. Bake in preheated oven 25 to 30 minutes or until golden brown. Cool completely in pan on a wire rack.
4. To make topping, melt chocolate and butter or margarine in a small heavy saucepan over very low heat; stir until smooth. Let cool.
5. Remove cooled muesli mixture from pan; peel off foil. Place on a flat surface; spread chocolate mixture over top. Let stand until chocolate is set. Cut into 16 bars. Makes 16 cookies.

Muesli was one of the best known items in the raw-food diet devised by Switzerland's Dr. Bircher-Brenner in the 1930's. He originally intended the diet to be rich in fruit. The modern version contains a lot more cereal. Although muesli is best known as a breakfast food, it makes a good meal at any time when combined with fresh fruit and milk or yogurt. Muesli is made from a selection of cereals, such as rolled oats, cracked wheat, rye flakes, wheat germ and bran. Dried fruits, nuts and sometimes sugar are added to this base. Muesli is available in some supermarkets and specialty shops.

Rum & Chocolate Cake

SWITZERLAND

1 recipe Cocoa Layer Cake, page 51
Syrup:
1 cup water
1/2 cup firmly packed light-brown sugar
2 tablespoons unsweetened cocoa powder
1/4 cup dark rum

Filling:
4 oz. semisweet chocolate, chopped
2 tablespoons whipping cream
1 egg, beaten
1 teaspoon vanilla extract
Powdered sugar

---

1. Preheat oven to 350F (175C). Grease 2 (8-inch) round cake pans. Prepare and bake Cocoa Layer Cake as directed on page 51.
2. Cool cake layers in pans on wire racks 5 minutes. Remove from pans; cool completely on wire racks.
3. To make syrup, in a small saucepan over low heat, combine water, brown sugar and cocoa. Cook, stirring, until sugar dissolves. Bring to a boil. Remove from heat; stir in rum.
4. Wash and dry cake pans. Return cake layers to clean pans, top-side up. Poke holes in top of each layer with a fork or metal skewer. Spoon syrup over layers; let stand 2 to 3 hours.
5. To make filling, melt chocolate in a small heavy saucepan over very low heat; stir until smooth. Whisk in cream, egg and vanilla until mixture is smooth. Cool slightly; refrigerate until completely cool and almost firm.
6. Remove cake layers from pans; place 1 layer, bottom-side up, on a serving plate. Spread with cooled chocolate filling; top with second layer, bottom-side down.
7. Place a lace doily on top of cake; sift powdered sugar over doily. Carefully remove doily. Makes 6 to 8 servings.

Top to bottom: Rum & Chocolate Cake, Chocolate-Muesli Bars

Index